Your Nation to Save

YOUR NATION TO SAVE

A LINE-BY-LINE EXPLANATION OF THE US CONSTITUTION

Tatjana —

Be courageous, involved, + informed!

Shane F. Krauser 1/22/13

SHANE F. KRAUSER

Your Nation to Save: A Line-by-Line Explanation of the US Constitution
Published by the American Academy for Constitutional Education in Gilbert, Arizona
www.aafce.com

Nothing in this book is prescriptive or intended as legal advice, and readers should consult competent professionals for such advice.

Cover design and typesetting by Susan Veach
Edited by Sandra Udall Crandall

For information, contact info@aafce.com.

Printed and bound in the United States of America

For wholesale and bulk discounts for educational, business, fundraising, and sales promotional use, contact info@aafce.com.

ISBN 978-0-9850540-0-7

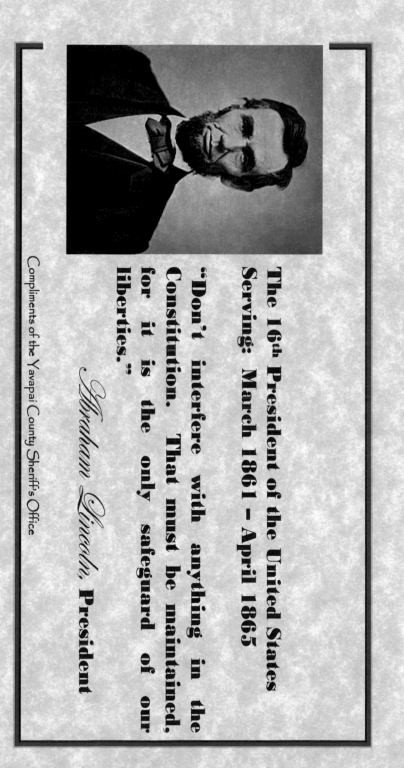

The 16th President of the United States
Serving: March 1861 – April 1865

"Don't interfere with anything in the Constitution. That must be maintained, for it is the only safeguard of our liberties."

Abraham Lincoln, President

*To the inspiration of all inspirations
and the reason why I love America—namely, my family,
including my beautiful wife, Janelle;
our five sons, Ammon, Daniel, Jacob, Fenton, and Aidan;
our daughter, Shanelle;
and my father and mother, Richard and Erna Arnold.*

The Constitution text came from the Federal Government Archives website.

Table of Contents

Foreword

By Congressman Matt Salmon

Shane Krauser's work, *Your Nation to Save*, is sorely needed in America right here and right now. Our government and our leaders over time have gradually moved us away from the very framework that sets us apart from all other nations of the world. And the results are staggering. We have runaway deficits, massive debt, and a top-heavy and bloated federal government. And that just scratches the surface.

As Mr. Krauser so aptly points out in *Your Nation to Save*, we waste so much time arguing and debating in terms of the "Left" versus the "Right." In fact, we would far better solve what ails us if we changed the debate to "constitutional" versus "unconstitutional." The daunting fiscal problem we face as a nation today would be solved if our leaders would remove laws, agencies, and appropriations that are not strictly provided for in the Constitution. And the best way to elect constitutionally-minded leaders is to have a voting public who understands the Constitution as well.

Mr. Krauser has become a tireless advocate and educator of this blessed document to anyone who will listen. God bless him for his efforts because an educated public on these matters is really the only thing that will get us back on track. Please read and study this guide, and give one or two or ten to your friends. The time is now! Let's take our country back and get back to the blueprint for success drafted for us by inspired and enlightened individuals over two centuries ago. Our very future hangs in the balance.

Preface

Make no mistake about it—freedom in America hangs precariously in the balance, and Americans are engaging in a battle for liberty with an intensity that has not existed since the 1770s. The reality of the circumstances made clear by Thomas Paine in 1776 applies today just as well: "These are the times that try men's souls." We, the people, must rise up like never before, acknowledge that this is a battle worth fighting, and recognize that freedom still works. You are indispensable to this effort, which means *you* must fully engage and make the case for freedom. Not somebody else—*you* must make the case.

Like each and every individual in this country, you must make some critical and profound choices: Will you be a free citizen who enjoys the rewards of liberty or a slave who desires to have the government make decisions for you? If you wish to be free, what will you do to restore freedom in America in the face of ongoing government overreaching into almost every facet of our lives? What will you do to change the attitude in this country that "all is lost" and that government officials—most of whom lack a clear understanding of what freedom really is—will continue to abuse their power regardless of the demands of the people? These are important questions that carry with them heavy implications.

The empowering news is that there is a solution, and it is going to require people who are as courageous as James Madison, as stalwart as George Washington, and as persistent as Thomas Jefferson. If your choice is for liberty, doing nothing is not an option. If your choice is for liberty, this book will give you the ammunition to do something—something powerful!

America needs technicians of the Constitution—people who experience liberty at their inner core and understand, articulate, and put freedom and its protection into practice in order to preserve the great American experiment. America needs people who have the vision of the patriots who risked it all on the shores of the Delaware River with nothing but burlap on their feet (1776), at Long Island where the fight was on even though outnumbered (1776), and at Yorktown where the American spirit prevailed (1781). Today, America needs people who have the courage to defend this country's foundation at town hall meetings and community events, who have the confidence to believe that their voice will make a difference, and who have the conviction to converse with people of all backgrounds about the relevancy of the Constitution.

Your Nation to Save will empower you and change the way you see and understand the Constitution. This book will break the Constitution down in ways that will allow you to digest it in rather simple terms. As you proceed, it will become clear that the Constitution is not the problem. It is emphatically the answer, and nearly all of the ills in this country can be solved by strict adherence to its text, intent, and purpose.

Many people are overwhelmed and even intimidated by the proposition of reading and trying to understand the Constitution. This book is designed to help the average American understand its general principles, its demands, and its protections. Any individual reading this book will come away understanding more about the Constitution than 90% of the American population. Not only is it empowering to study, embrace, and spread freedom's message, it is what patriots once did just as a matter of course. And it is not just a privilege for Americans to be a part of this great cause. It is an obligation, a duty, and a sacred honor.

How to Use This Book

This is a line-by-line explanation of the US Constitution put together to allow you to see the original intent, language, and structure, along with where and how changes have been made. As you proceed through this book, note a few things about structure:

On the left side of each page, you will see the Constitution in its original form. On the right side of each page, you will see the explanation of each constitutional provision. In addition, you will see some provisions of the original Constitution that are underlined, which means that this particular portion has been made obsolete in some way, shape, or form.

This book still gives an explanation of the original, now-obsolete version and gives further reference for understanding that provision, such as where those nullified versions were amended or where it addresses the provision in further detail.

So, here we go. As you proceed to study this document—the great protector of freedom—may the words of Thomas Paine permeate your heart and mind: "The summer soldier and the sunshine patriot will, in this crisis, shrink from the service of their country; but he that stands it now, deserves the love and thanks of man and woman." We owe this effort to those who have gone before us and to those who have yet to come. This is *Your Nation to Save!*

Your Nation to Save

Freedom secured at a heavy price can only be retained by a people who understand what was ultimately secured. The Declaration of Independence outlines the many reasons our founding fathers were willing to pledge everything—their lives, their fortunes, and their sacred honor. Indeed, it is the greatest manifesto on human rights ever written. It persuasively argues the case for freedom, and it is the "why" of this great American experiment.

As our founders risked everything to set this experiment in motion, they recognized, first and foremost, that human beings were made to be free. The human experience was to allow every man and woman to make choices free from government interference—to be responsible for their own choices and not have the government make fundamental decisions for them. The founders struggled and wrestled with how to balance the freedom of individuals with the need for an orderly society where the freedom of one could not infringe on the freedom of others.

As they moved towards this ideal, they recognized something profound that would be the basis for our government—every person, simply by virtue of their humanity, is endowed with certain unalienable rights that no human being could bestow upon them or take away. This, of course, means that the government is not the source of our rights. The government is not even the source of the authority to act on behalf of any given society. Rights begin with the very essence of our humanity, and the power to govern begins with the people. The men and women who declared independence from tyranny, the abuse of power, and nonexistent representation recognized these truths, and they were willing to risk the gallows.

America is not perfect. She never has been and never will be because, as James Madison observed, men are not angels. The Constitution establishes and permits the pursuit of an ideal that is unique in the annals of history. It anticipates the imperfections of man and the shortcomings of government institutions by solidifying powerful, long-standing principles and concepts that are essential to a free society, such as the separation of powers, division of authority, limited government, the amendment process, and the primacy of the individual.

One can only really understand America if they understand where she came from, what struggles she endured, and the common objective that so many fought for. A country is only as good as her people, and America is no different. Imagine going back to the halls of Philadelphia in 1787 when this country was literally on the brink of disaster. Americans should understand what our founders were so fearlessly confronting, why they debated endlessly for months, and why individuals often went into long-winded tirades and "speechified" for hours. They all understood liberty, and they all wanted to maximize its exercise and ensure that tyranny could never place a vice grip on the people again. These men were serious about liberty because they had experienced oppression. And they refused to remain silent.

We have inherited this great experiment, and we must understand what was bargained and settled for and the essence of the governmental system established. We must see oppression and its consequences through the founder's eyes, and their watchful eyes must become our eyes. Their voice must become our voice. We must be vigilant in maintaining and guarding freedom and ensure, as George Washington admonished, that principles always supersede party affiliation. We must be beholden to freedom first and foremost. Unfortunately, America has often times deviated from this wisdom.

PRINCIPLES OVER PARTY –
THE PROPER FORM OF GOVERNMENT

America has been negotiating freedom and the proper form of government for over two centuries now. Sadly, the party system controls America, pigeonholes an individual into one particular philosophy, and has done little to protect freedom. It is more often part of the problem than the solution.

We often use the terms "Left" and "Right" to define political philosophies and ideology. However, this system of defining political systems is inept, for it tells us little to nothing about the function of government. As my father often said, "The extreme right and extreme left are actually more similar than most think. They both have agendas but are both set on obtaining more power to secure that agenda." While the Right may be interested in embracing traditional values, the free market system, and deregulation of businesses and the Left advocates protecting the working class, regulating certain industries, and the preservation of certain fundamental liberties, both are interested in more power to achieve their objectives. This grasping for power, in practice, means less liberty for everyone. And this goes directly to the point that party politics rarely addresses the proper scope of government operation. While it may allow the individual to attempt to describe his or her political philosophies, it is wholly inadequate for restoring America because, unfortunately, political agendas too often supersede the ideal.

The proper way to analyze government or even the scope of any idea presented is first recognizing the two extremes that revolve around power. Why? Because it is power that always threatens freedom. On one extreme is tyranny, which is "too much government power" and which always places a stranglehold on freedom. Because human beings in power tend to seek more power, it often comes at the expense of the people and their liberty. The other extreme is anarchy, which is "too little government power" and leads to freedom for a few and the suppression of freedom for most. As things get out of hand under an anarchy, which they always do, factions will rise up and lead to an oligarchy—namely, rule by a few people.

Neither one of these extremes is sufficient to allow society as a whole to enjoy freedom. The objective is to find middle ground between tyranny and anarchy—to have a government big enough to protect the liberties of the people, yet small enough to ensure that government infringements on those liberties are kept to an absolute minimum. The Constitution, in its purest form, does this remarkably well. We, as citizens of the United States of America, are incredibly fortunate.

THE GREATNESS OF AMERICA REMAINS IN HER PEOPLE

The purpose of the Constitution must once again become the central theme of our political climate. While many citizens do not understand its purpose, there is nothing mysterious about its design and intent. This country's problems can only be resolved by statesmen and the American people understanding how this document protects liberty, restrains and limits power, and ensures the power lies with the people.

No other document protects liberty the way the US Constitution does, and no other document has withstood the test of time like it has. Just as the Declaration of the Independence is the "why" of this great American experiment, the Constitution is the "how" and was written in order to preserve and protect freedom on a scale never before experienced. It is because of the Constitution that the United States is the greatest country established in the entire history of the world. It was founded on something more than clichés, sound bites, buzzwords, and vague ideology. Instead, it is and was based on sound principles of liberty, a firm understanding of the consequences of placing power in the hands of individuals, and a nonnegotiable recognition of where the power to govern begins—with the people. America can remain great so long as the people commit to maintaining its foundation and the framework that is designed to govern, namely the Constitution. As Thomas Paine once said, "Those who enjoy the blessings of freedom must, like men, undergo the fatigue of supporting it."

The beauty of America is that her problems can be fixed by utilizing and honoring the tools already in place. Those tools have preserved certain ideas and, at the same time, allowed enhanced protection of the individual. For example, we enjoy a peaceful transition of power because our Constitution specifically provides for such a transition. There is no bloodshed or guesswork that accompanies the passing of the torch. Similarly, individuals, regardless of race or gender, are permitted to vote through a Constitution that provides for the amendment process. In addition, other political systems have not been able to trump our Constitution because the Constitution declares that it is the "supreme law of the land." These are just a few examples.

So, if the Constitution is the answer, where have we gone wrong? The answer is simple—we the people have been diverted and have focused on everything but the real issue.

THE PROBLEMS IN AMERICA CAN BE FIXED

The Constitution provides for an election process, which not only means we are able to decide who will represent us, but also means we have the ability to hold our elected officials accountable. An uninformed electorate can wreak havoc on our system and place our constitutional government into disarray. This is precisely where the train has derailed.

The electorate has ultimately put people in power who are either ignorant of or blatantly disregard the principles outlined in the Constitution. The Constitution provides limited authority for government officials to act. In other words, officials cannot legislate in whatever areas they please. Instead, they must operate within the parameters outlined in the Constitution. Unfortunately, this has not happened.

Many Americans would be surprised to discover that Congress, for example, legislates and controls the production, manufacture, and sale of consumer goods like washing machines, light bulbs, faucets, balloons, latex gloves, marbles, rattles, lawnmowers, pool slides, matchboxes, fitness equipment, and even toilets. And this just touches the surface of unconstitutional congressional conduct. In the executive branch, it is not uncommon for the president to avoid the legislative process, making his or her own laws through issuing executive orders. Generally, the citizenry —and Congress—doesn't even bat an eye at such action. The judicial branch has interpreted the Constitution, in many cases, clearly outside the scope of its original intent and, in doing so, has created its own laws—usurping the power of the legislative branch and lashing out at freedom. The judicial branch has gone so far as to prohibit a farmer from growing wheat on his own land for his own consumption and told businesses how many hours their employees may work, thus infringing on the fundamental right to contract. Suffice it say that we have permitted Congress, the president, and our courts to act in impermissible ways.

Most don't question the government's unconstitutional runaway train, primarily because we don't know or are unable to identify the unconstitutional conduct. In the words of Benjamin Franklin, "It is in the regions of ignorance that tyranny begins." As we educate ourselves as to the proper scope of government authority and commit ourselves to the principles of the Constitution, we are better able to articulate our own political opinions and be a force for good. Vigilance is a major component of the solution.

THE CONSTITUTION:
SEPARATE, LIMIT, AND PROTECT

There is a reason our Constitution is the model to our neighbors worldwide as to the proper form of government. Let's talk about the most profound components:

- Our Constitution recognizes the primacy of the individual and the principle of popular sovereignty. In other words, the people can govern themselves and the power through which anyone governs comes from the people.

- The division of power ensures that no one branch obtains too much power, and this concern is further tempered by giving the various branches of government specified authority to perform certain functions. In other words, a brilliant system of checks and balances is created.

- Our government is a limited government. The authority that is not granted to the federal government is ultimately retained by the states and the people. Within this separation, there are limitations on what the government can do.

- The enumeration of rights in our Constitution via some provisions in the body of the Constitution, as well as the various amendments, puts the government on notice as to the recognition of certain rights and notifies government that these rights are to be protected. Again, the Declaration of Independence makes it very clear that government has but one primary purpose: "[T]o secure these rights, governments are instituted among men."

Our Constitution is unique. As one begins to understand it, defending it becomes a joy and a privilege.

OVERVIEW OF THE US CONSTITUTION

Here is a brief overview of our Constitution. As you will see and as previously noted, the Constitution divides and limits authority, separates power, and mandates that government stay out of the people's business and intervene only to prevent the abuse of the rights of the individuals or when rights are potentially being infringed upon—a task which cannot be taken lightly. Further, you should know that this Constitution is, for the most part, a compact between the people or the states and the federal government. Maintaining this relationship has been one of the ongoing struggles of this country.

Article I (Legislative Authority) – The legislative branch of government is given approximately 20 powers. Congress may only act within the scope of these powers, which are found in Article I, Section 8. Further restrictions on the federal government are found in Article I, Section 9, while state restrictions are found in Article I, Section 10.

Article II (Executive Authority) – The President is given but a few specific powers, and he or she may only act within these specified powers.

Article III (Judicial Authority) – The federal courts are limited to the types of cases they may hear. They may not exceed their enumerated jurisdiction and authority.

Article IV (Relationships Among the States) – This article discusses the full faith and credit clause, how a state becomes a member of the union, extradition procedures, and the states' guarantee of a republican form of government.

Article V (Amendment Process) – While Articles I, II, and III provide horizontal checks within the three branches of government, Article V provides a vertical check by allowing the "people" to amend the Constitution. In addition, Congress may facilitate amendments, and the process of doing so has some general guidelines.

Article VI (Supremacy) – In addition to addressing federal debt at the time of the country's founding, the oath of office, and the prohibition against a religious test for federal office, the Constitution declares that it is the supreme law of the land.

Article VII (Ratification) – Listed here are the constitutional ratification procedures, which required nine of the thirteen original states to ratify in order for the Constitution to become the supreme document.

Twenty-Seven Amendments – These various amendments expand and further limit government power, as well as protect and solidify the rights of the people.

All three branches of government have an obligation to uphold the Constitution. When one branch moves into action, others may *potentially* intervene on some level. This form of government represents a true republic, where the government is limited to advancing and maintaining certain areas that are delegated to them. As a result, the people have an obligation to elect solid leaders who understand these principles. Individuals who are elected should also understand this. If they do, they are more like to tread delicately, for they will recognize that our liberty is at stake, and it is their job to secure it.

Preamble

We the People of the United States, in Order to form a more perfect Union, establish Justice, insure domestic Tranquility, provide for the common defence, promote the general Welfare, and secure the Blessings of Liberty to ourselves and our Posterity, do ordain and establish this Constitution for the United States of America.

_____

_____

_____

_____

_____

_____

_____

_____

_____

_____

_____

_____

Purpose

Recognizing their inalienable and inherent right to govern themselves, the people of the United States created the Constitution for the following reasons:

1. To form a strong central government made up of a union of states that are joined together by a common purpose.
2. To ensure equal and just treatment to all through the principles of due process and fairness.
3. To ensure peace within America's borders.
4. To protect the people of the United States against foreign and domestic enemies.
5. To meet the needs of the general population in order to allow society to function free from government or even private interference. Note here that promoting the general welfare is different than providing for the general welfare. The government has an obligation to the former but not the latter.
6. To ensure liberty from one generation to the next.

Notes

_____

_____

_____

_____

_____

_____

_____

Article. I.

SECTION. 1.

All legislative Powers herein granted shall be vested in a Congress of the United States, which shall consist of a Senate and House of Representatives.

_____

_____

_____

_____

_____

_____

_____

_____

_____

_____

Article I
(Powers of the Legislative Branch)

Section 1 (Legislative Powers Vested in the House of Representatives and the Senate)

Article I of the Constitution primarily addresses the lawmaking function of the legislative branch. Section 1 establishes a few important principles:

1. The legislative branch holds the lawmaking authority. Because lawmaking is a vested power, it cannot be delegated.
2. The legislature consists of the lower house (House of Representatives) and the upper house (Senate).
3. The powers of the legislative branch are limited to the powers specifically enumerated in the Constitution itself (i.e., if the authority is not specifically granted through the Constitution, the Tenth Amendment ensures that the power is reserved to the states and to the people). The powers delegated to the legislative branch are few and defined.

SECTION. 2.

The House of Representatives shall be composed of Members chosen every second Year by the People of the several States, and the Electors in each State shall have the Qualifications requisite for Electors of the most numerous Branch of the State Legislature.

No Person shall be a Representative who shall not have attained to the Age of twenty five Years, and been seven Years a Citizen of the United States, and who shall not, when elected, be an Inhabitant of that State in which he shall be chosen.

Representatives and direct Taxes shall be apportioned among the several States which may be included within this Union, according to their respective Numbers, which shall be determined by adding to the whole Number of free Persons, including those bound to Service for a Term of Years, and excluding Indians not taxed, three fifths of all other Persons.

The actual Enumeration shall be made within three Years after the first Meeting of the Congress of the United States, and within every subsequent

SECTION 2 (HOUSE OF REPRESENTATIVES)

The voters of the separate states elect the members of the House of Representatives every two years. The House of Representatives was to be the only part of the US government to be elected directly by the people. The Constitution does not dictate voting eligibility requirements. It only mandates that any person who is deemed qualified to vote for the various state legislatures be considered qualified to vote for the members of the House of Representatives.

In order to seek election to the House of Representatives, a person must be at least twenty-five years old, a citizen of the United States for at least seven years, and an inhabitant of the state in which they are seeking election. Notably, the Constitution makes no mention of term limits for the House of Representatives.

This section was changed by Section 2 of the Fourteenth Amendment and the Sixteenth Amendment. Nevertheless, this subsection provided that the number of representatives from each state that would comprise the House of Representatives would be determined by population. Hence, larger states would have more representation than smaller states. However, those larger states would also be responsible for paying more taxes in the form of direct taxes (taxation primarily on property). Finally, for the purpose of determining the population of each state, every person would be counted as a "whole person" except slaves (i.e., non-free persons) and American Indians who did not pay taxes. Slaves would be counted as three-fifths of one person.

This clause guarantees the individual's right to be represented in the House of Representatives. That representation hinges on the population of the particular state relative to the other states.

Term of ten Years, in such Manner as they shall by Law direct. The Number of Representatives shall not exceed one for every thirty Thousand, but each State shall have at Least one Representative; and until such enumeration shall be made, the State of New Hampshire shall be entitled to chuse three, Massachusetts eight, Rhode-Island and Providence Plantations one, Connecticut five, New-York six, New Jersey four, Pennsylvania eight, Delaware one, Maryland six, Virginia ten, North Carolina five, South Carolina five, and Georgia three.

When vacancies happen in the Representation from any State, the Executive Authority thereof shall issue Writs of Election to fill such Vacancies.

The House of Representatives shall chuse their Speaker and other Officers; and shall have the sole Power of Impeachment.

The greater the population of a state, the greater the representation. A census is required in order to determine the total number of representatives each state should have in Congress. The first census was to be taken within three years after the first meeting of Congress and every ten years thereafter. Each state would have at least one representative, but in order to avoid too many members, representation would never amount to more than one per 30,000 people. Prior to the first census, the states were allotted the following representation: New Hampshire – 3; Massachusetts – 8; Rhode Island – 1; Connecticut – 5; New York – 6; New Jersey – 4; Pennsylvania – 8; Delaware – 1; Maryland – 6; Virginia – 10; North Carolina – 5; South Carolina – 5; Georgia – 3. As of 2011, the total number of representatives is fixed at 435. This number may be modified by Congress.

When a member of the House of Representatives does not finish his or her two-year term due to resignation, death, or any other reason, the governor of the state will determine the election process for the replacement.

The members of the House of Representatives have the power to choose their speaker, which is the highest office within the legislative branch, as well as other officers who assist in carrying out the law-making function. In addition, the House of Representatives has the sole power of impeachment—only they can bring the impeachment charges or indictment against a member of the executive or judicial branch. To further understand the power of impeachment, refer to Article I, Section 3, which designates the Senate as the body that will actually hear and adjudicate the case, establishes the procedures to be used for such a trial, and specifies punishment. In addition, Article I, Section 4 sets forth who may be an impeached and upon what grounds, and Article II, Section 2 prevents the president from issuing pardons in cases of impeachment.

SECTION. 3.

The Senate of the United States shall be composed of two Senators from each State, <u>chosen by the Legislature</u> thereof for six Years; and each Senator shall have one Vote.

Immediately after they shall be assembled in Consequence of the first Election, they shall be divided as equally as may be into three Classes. The Seats of the Senators of the first Class shall be vacated at the Expiration of the second Year, of the second Class at the Expiration of the fourth Year, and of the third Class at the Expiration of the sixth Year, so that one third may be chosen every second Year;

<u>and if Vacancies happen by Resignation, or otherwise, during the Recess of the Legislature of any State, the Executive thereof may make temporary Appointments until the next Meeting of the Legislature, which shall then fill such Vacancies.</u>

No Person shall be a Senator who shall not have attained to the Age of thirty Years, and been nine Years a Citizen of the United States, and who shall

SECTION 3 (SENATE)

Each state has equal representation in the Senate. Every state has two senators, each of which serves a six-year term and has one vote in the Senate. While the foregoing is still accurate today, the process through which a person becomes a senator has changed. The process has been revised by the Seventeenth Amendment. Originally, this clause required that the state legislatures appoint two senators. The Seventeenth Amendment changed this to allow the people to elect the senators.

This provision rotates the terms of office for senators so that the entire Senate is not up for reelection at the same time. The first meeting or "class" of elected senators required the division of senators into three groups: one which would end its initial term at the end of the second year, another group would end its term at the end of the fourth year, and the third group would end its term at the end of the sixth year. After these initial terms by the first incoming class of senators, the terms would continue for all senators for a period of six years. This would ensure that no more than one-third of the Senate would be elected every two years and would preserve the continuity of the Senate as a political body.

When a senator does not finish his or her term, the governor from the senator's state must establish a special election to fill the vacancy. This clause was changed by the Seventeenth Amendment. Now, when a vacancy in the Senate occurs, the governor may appoint a replacement who serves until a special election is called or until the next general election, as specified by the state legislature.

The minimum age for a senator is thirty, and the minimum length of US citizenship is nine years. When elected, a senator must be a resident of the state he or she is seek-

not, when elected, be an Inhabitant of that State for which he shall be chosen.

The Vice President of the United States shall be President of the Senate, but shall have no Vote, unless they be equally divided.

The Senate shall chuse their other Officers, and also a President pro tempore, in the Absence of the Vice President, or when he shall exercise the Office of President of the United States.

The Senate shall have the sole Power to try all Impeachments. When sitting for that Purpose, they shall be on Oath or Affirmation. When the President of the United States is tried, the Chief Justice shall preside: And no Person shall be convicted without the Concurrence of two thirds of the Members present.

Judgment in Cases of Impeachment shall not extend further than to removal from Office, and dis-

ing to represent. The age and citizenship requirements must be reached before a senator is sworn in and not necessarily at the time of election. Notably, the Constitution makes no mention of term limits for the Senate.

The vice president is given the position of the president of the Senate, but he or she may only vote in the event of a tie. The ability to vote under these circumstances is one of the checks and balances that the executive branch has on the legislative branch. The vice president is the only government official who is a member of two branches of government: the legislative and the executive. According to the Twelfth Amendment, the vice president is next in line for the presidency but is otherwise given no specific executive duties.

The Senate has the power to choose officers who will work with them in carrying out their legislative functions. One specific officer is the president pro tempore (aka president pro tem), who presides when the vice president is absent. According the Twenty-fifth Amendment, the president pro tem is third in the line of succession to the presidency, after the vice president and the Speaker of the House.

Once the House of Representatives has impeached an official (Article I, Section 2), the Senate holds a trial to determine guilt or innocence and must take an oath of impartiality. The House appoints individuals who act as prosecutors, and the accused may be represented by counsel. Senators act as the jurors, and no conviction may result unless two-thirds of the members present vote for it. In cases where the US president is tried for impeachment, the chief justice of the United States Supreme Court presides over the proceeding.

The maximum penalty resulting from impeachment is the removal from office and a bar from holding a position

qualification to hold and enjoy any Office of honor, Trust or Profit under the United States: but the Party convicted shall nevertheless be liable and subject to Indictment, Trial, Judgment and Punishment, according to Law.

Notes

within the United States government. The Senate votes on each of these issues independently. Regardless of whether the Senate convicts or acquits, the official is still subject to criminal accountability for their conduct, which does not violate the "double jeopardy" clause of the Fifth Amendment.

Notes

_____

_____

_____

_____

_____

_____

_____

_____

_____

_____

_____

_____

_____

SECTION. 4.

The Times, Places and Manner of holding Elections for Senators and Representatives, shall be prescribed in each State by the Legislature thereof; but the Congress may at any time by Law make or alter such Regulations, except as to the Places of chusing Senators.

The Congress shall assemble at least once in every Year, and such Meeting shall be on the first Monday in December, unless they shall by Law appoint a different Day.

Notes

SECTION 4 (CONGRESSIONAL ELECTIONS AND MEETING REQUIREMENTS)

The various state legislatures have the power to regulate the times, places, and manner of elections for both members of the Senate and the House of Representatives. However, Congress may override those procedures and determine the process under which votes are cast by the people. Congress may not override the decisions of the states as to the location of the elections.

Unless Congress changes the date by passing a new law, Congress is required to meet at least once per year, beginning on the first Monday in December. While Congress is still required to meet once annually, the date for meeting was changed by the Twentieth Amendment, which established the actual meeting date as January 3, unless the legislature sets a different date by law.

Notes

SECTION. 5.

Each House shall be the Judge of the Elections, Returns and Qualifications of its own Members, and a Majority of each shall constitute a Quorum to do Business; but a smaller Number may adjourn from day to day, and may be authorized to compel the Attendance of absent Members, in such Manner, and under such Penalties as each House may provide.

Each House may determine the Rules of its Proceedings, punish its Members for disorderly Behaviour, and, with the Concurrence of two thirds, expel a Member. Each House shall keep a Journal of its Proceedings, and from time to time publish the same, excepting such Parts as may in their Judgment require Secrecy; and the Yeas and Nays of the Members of either House on any question shall, at the Desire of one fifth of those Present, be entered on the Journal.

Neither House, during the Session of Congress, shall, without the Consent of the other, adjourn for more than three days, nor to any other Place than that in which the two Houses shall be sitting.

SECTION 5 (CONGRESSIONAL RULES OF ORDER)

Both the House of Representatives and the Senate have the power to determine the elections, returns, and qualifications of its own members. In other words, each house has the power to determine whether its members were properly elected and whether they meet the required qualifications. In order for each respective house to conduct business, a quorum of its members must be present, which consists of a majority of the total members. If there are not enough members present to constitute a quorum, the smaller group may meet. This smaller group may compel the attendance of other members and also determine the penalty for a member's failure to appear according to the rules established by each house.

Each house may establish rules regarding how it will conduct business and engage in the legislative process. In addition, each house may punish its members for unruly or disorderly conduct. Upon a two-thirds vote, they may remove a member from office. Each house is required to keep an official record of its proceedings in order to allow the public to know what legislative actions have been taken. If deemed necessary, each house may keep certain actions secret. If one-fifth of those present request it, the member's individual yea or nay vote on any bill will be recorded in the official record of the house to which the government official belongs.

When Congress is in session, neither the House of Representatives nor the Senate may adjourn for more than three days without the other's consent. A change of venue or location by either house can only be done with the consent of the other. Both houses must coordinate their schedules to ensure that legislative measures are not delayed.

SECTION. 6.

The Senators and Representatives shall receive a Compensation for their Services, to be ascertained by Law, and paid out of the Treasury of the United States.

They shall in all Cases, except Treason, Felony and Breach of the Peace, be privileged from Arrest during their Attendance at the Session of their respective Houses, and in going to and returning from the same; and for any Speech or Debate in either House, they shall not be questioned in any other Place.

No Senator or Representative shall, during the Time for which he was elected, be appointed to any civil Office under the Authority of the United States, which shall have been created, or the Emoluments whereof shall have been encreased during such time; and no Person holding any Office under the United States, shall be a Member of either House during his Continuance in Office.

SECTION 6 (CONGRESSIONAL PAY, IMMUNITIES, AND OFFICE PROHIBITION)

Congress is to be paid by the US government out of the national treasury and not by the states. According to the Twenty-seventh Amendment, any changes in the senators' or representatives' salary may not take place until after the next election of the members of each house—namely, the Senate and the House of Representatives.

The legislature enjoys two kinds of immunities. First, members of both houses are immune from arrest for civil or petty offenses, such as the payment of debt, but they can be arrested for misdemeanors, felonies, and treason. Second, legislators are immune from arrest for comments made as a function of the legislative process. This protects legislators from lawsuits brought as a result of their speech that is essential to the deliberative function of lawmaking. Both types of immunities protect the legislators when traveling to or from the legislative session or while participating in a legislative session.

Members of Congress may not assume a federal office that was created during his or her term or for which the salary was increased. As a result, legislators may not directly benefit from appointments outside of the legislative branch. This clause ensures the separation of powers in that no member of Congress can simultaneously hold an office in the executive or judicial branches.

SECTION. 7.

All Bills for raising Revenue shall originate in the House of Representatives; but the Senate may propose or concur with Amendments as on other Bills.

Every Bill which shall have passed the House of Representatives and the Senate, shall, before it become a Law, be presented to the President of the United States: If he approve he shall sign it, but if not he shall return it, with his Objections to that House in which it shall have originated, who shall enter the Objections at large on their Journal, and proceed to reconsider it.

If after such Reconsideration two thirds of that House shall agree to pass the Bill, it shall be sent, together with the Objections, to the other House, by which it shall likewise be reconsidered, and if approved by two thirds of that House, it shall become a Law.

But in all such Cases the Votes of both Houses shall be determined by yeas and Nays, and the Names of the Persons voting for and against the Bill shall be entered on the Journal of each House respectively. If any Bill shall not be returned by the President within ten Days (Sundays excepted) after it shall have been presented to him, the Same shall be a Law, in like Manner as if he had signed it, unless the Congress by their Adjournment prevent its Return, in which Case it shall not be a Law.

Section 7 (Congressional Law-Making Procedure)

Bills, or proposed legislative action, related to raising money must originate in the House of Representatives. However, the Senate may propose additional action or simply agree just as they may do with other bills that are not related to revenue measures.

Every bill passed by both houses must be presented to the president for his approval. If he approves of the bill, he must sign it in order for it to become law. However, if he disagrees with the proposed law, he must return it, along with his objections, to the house in which the proposed law originated. That house must then enter any objections to the bill and then proceed to reconsider any of those objections or proposed changes.

If, upon reconsidering the law, two-thirds of the members of the house that initiated the law agree to pass it, they send it to the other house for reconsideration. If that house also approves the proposed law by a two-thirds vote, it will become law without the president's approval.

In every case where a law is proposed, the names of each individual voting for ("yea") or against ("nay") the bill must be recorded in the legislative journal. If any proposed piece of legislation is delivered to the president for signing and is not returned by the president within ten days with his or her signature approving of the bill (not counting Sundays), it will become law. The one exception to the president failing to sign and return revolves around the legislature making the delivery impossible by adjourning during the ten-day period. In this case, the proposed legislation will not become law.

Every Order, Resolution, or Vote to which the Concurrence of the Senate and House of Representatives may be necessary (except on a question of Adjournment) shall be presented to the President of the United States; and before the Same shall take Effect, shall be approved by him, or being disapproved by him, shall be repassed by two thirds of the Senate and House of Representatives, according to the Rules and Limitations prescribed in the Case of a Bill.

This clause ensures that the president participates in the legislative process. In every case where an order, resolution, or vote takes place that requires the agreement of both the House and Senate, the president must approve it before it can take effect. In cases where the president vetoes (does not approve) of the bill, it must be sent back to both houses and must be approved by a two-thirds vote of both houses in order to take effect. This clause does not apply to a vote to adjourn or to proposed constitutional amendments. Proposed constitutional amendments do not have to be approved by the president before they are sent to the states for ratification.

Notes

_____

_____

_____

_____

_____

_____

_____

_____

_____

_____

SECTION. 8.

The Congress shall have Power

To lay and collect Taxes, Duties, Imposts and Excises, to pay the Debts and provide for the common Defence and general Welfare of the United States; but all Duties, Imposts and Excises shall be uniform throughout the United States;

To borrow Money on the credit of the United States;

To regulate Commerce with foreign Nations, and among the several States, and with the Indian Tribes;

SECTION 8 (ENUMERATED POWERS OF CONGRESS)

The following enumerated powers are delegated to Congress. The Tenth Amendment requires that the powers not outlined here or elsewhere in the Constitution be retained by the states and by the people.

Congress has the power to collect taxes from the people and the states. They also have the authority to collect indirect taxes, such as duties (tax on imports, exports, or manufactured goods), imposts (tax on imports), and excises (federal sales tax). All of these taxes must be uniform throughout the United States. The collection of these taxes is to be utilized to pay the debts of the United States, provide for the defense of the entire nation, and to expend money for the welfare of the whole people or all of the member states. In other words, the federal taxes may not be levied for special interest groups or certain specific locales throughout the country.

Note: (1) The "general welfare" clause is not an independent power. Rather, it is directly linked to taxing and spending; and (2) All of the taxes noted here were considered indirect taxes and had to be applied uniformly. Direct taxes are addressed in Article I, Section 9 and required apportionment according to population of the states. This apportionment requirement was changed through the Sixteenth Amendment.

Congress is authorized to borrow money (create debt) on the credit of the United States.

Congress is authorized to regulate trade with foreign countries, between the separate states, and with the Indian tribes. Regulating commerce among the states involves ensuring free trade and movement of commerce between the states. No state may obstruct the free flow of commerce.

To establish an uniform Rule of Naturalization, and uniform Laws on the subject of Bankruptcies throughout the United States;

To coin Money, regulate the Value thereof, and of foreign Coin, and fix the Standard of Weights and Measures;

To provide for the Punishment of counterfeiting the Securities and current Coin of the United States;

To establish Post Offices and post Roads;

To promote the Progress of Science and useful Arts, by securing for limited Times to Authors and Inventors the exclusive Right to their respective Writings and Discoveries;

To constitute Tribunals inferior to the supreme Court;

Congress is authorized to establish the procedures for becoming a naturalized citizen and the laws that govern non-citizens entering the US. At the time of the ratification of the Constitution, citizenship was not defined. However, Section 1 of the Fourteenth Amendment addresses, in part, how a person may become a citizen of the United States. Congress is also authorized to establish uniform bankruptcy laws involving legal relief for debtors unable to pay their debts.

Congress has the exclusive power to coin money, which the states are prohibited from doing pursuant to Article I, Section 10. Congress also determines and regulates the value of domestic and foreign money and sets standard weights and measures.

Congress is authorized to establish the laws and punishment for the counterfeiting of paper money, coin, and securities (e.g., stocks and bonds).

Congress is authorized to establish post offices and postal roads, which is to ensure the speedy, consistent, and secure delivery of mail.

Congress is authorized to protect the copyright and patents of authors and inventors and to have their creative works (e.g., writings, discoveries, inventions, and other forms of intellectual property) protected under federal law for a designated period of time.

The right to petition the government for the redress of grievances is a protected right found in the First Amendment. Congress is authorized to set up a judicial system that allows for such petitions under the federal system. The US

To define and punish Piracies and Felonies committed on the high Seas, and Offences against the Law of Nations;

To declare War, grant Letters of Marque and Reprisal, and make Rules concerning Captures on Land and Water;

To raise and support Armies, but no Appropriation of Money to that Use shall be for a longer Term than two Years;

To provide and maintain a Navy;

To make Rules for the Government and Regulation of the land and naval Forces;

Supreme Court is established in Article III. However, the establishment of all lower federal courts, such as district and appellate courts, is left to Congress. (See also Article III, Section 1.)

Congress is authorized to define and punish those crimes that occur on the high seas, which are outside of the jurisdiction of the separate states. Congress is also authorized to the do the same for international crimes.

Congress is authorized to declare war and to grant letters of marque and reprisal (giving a private entity power to engage in an act of war or retaliation against the enemy). The states are specifically prohibited from declaring war (with certain exceptions) or granting letters of marque and reprisal according to Article I, Section 10. Congress also makes the laws concerning spoils of war made on land or water.

Congress is authorized to raise and support a national army. However, Congress may not raise money to fund that army for a term longer than two years (i.e., Congress must vote on military funding every two years). This provision is designed to, among other things, prevent a standing army and promote sound fiscal policy.

Congress is authorized to provide and maintain a naval force.

Congress is authorized to make the rules that govern land and naval military forces. Congress is also authorized to set up a different system of laws for the military that may vary from civil laws that exist for the general citizenry (e.g., criminal, contract, and tort law).

To provide for calling forth the Militia to execute the Laws of the Union, suppress Insurrections and repel Invasions;

To provide for organizing, arming, and disciplining, the Militia, and for governing such Part of them as may be employed in the Service of the United States, reserving to the States respectively, the Appointment of the Officers, and the Authority of training the Militia according to the discipline prescribed by Congress;

To exercise exclusive Legislation in all Cases whatsoever, over such District (not exceeding ten Miles square) as may, by Cession of particular States, and the Acceptance of Congress, become the Seat of the Government of the United States, and to exercise like Authority over all Places purchased by the Consent of the Legislature of the State in which the Same shall be, for the Erection of Forts, Magazines, Arsenals, dock-Yards, and other needful Buildings;--And

To make all Laws which shall be necessary and proper for carrying into Execution the foregoing Powers, and all other Powers vested by this Constitution in the Government of the United States, or in any Department or Officer thereof.

Congress has authority to determine how and when the state military forces (i.e., state militias, such as the National Guard) can be called into national service. These forces may be called up by the federal government in order to (1) execute the laws of the United States, such as the Constitution, federal law, and treaties; (2) to suppress rebellions and insurrections; and (3) repel invasions by those who would physically harm the United States.

Congress has the power to arm, equip, train, and establish rules for the state militias. However, the states reserve the right to appoint officers and implement the manner of military training as outlined by Congress.

Congress is authorized to set up a district, not to exceed ten square miles, as the seat of the federal government. Congress would enact all of the laws governing this locale, including criminal and civil laws. The land where this center would be located would be obtained from a state and would be independent altogether of the jurisdiction of any state government. This center is known today as Washington, DC. Congress would also have the same authority over forts, magazines, arsenals, dock-yards, and other buildings. These various entities would have to be located in areas that had been obtained or purchased from the separate states.

This provision is often referred to as the "elastic" clause because it grants Congress some flexibility in carrying out the specific, enumerated powers outlined in Article I, Section 8 or any other powers granted by the Constitution. The elastic clause is not an independent power but rather tied intricately to the enumerated powers of Congress.

SECTION. 9.

The Migration or Importation of such Persons as any of the States now existing shall think proper to admit, shall not be prohibited by the Congress prior to the Year one thousand eight hundred and eight, but a Tax or duty may be imposed on such Importation, not exceeding ten dollars for each Person.

The Privilege of the Writ of Habeas Corpus shall not be suspended, unless when in Cases of Rebellion or Invasion the public Safety may require it.

No Bill of Attainder or ex post facto Law shall be passed.

No Capitation, or other direct, Tax shall be laid, unless in Proportion to the Census or enumeration herein before directed to be taken.

SECTION 9 (CONGRESSIONAL PROHIBITIONS ON LEGISLATION)

Congress was prohibited from enacting any laws preventing the states from importing "persons" (i.e., immigrant, slave, or otherwise) until 1808. Congress was authorized to tax such importation in an amount not to exceed ten dollars per imported person. This clause is a direct result of the debate over the slave trade at the Constitutional Convention of 1787, and it carries no force of law today, as slavery was abolished by way of the Thirteenth Amendment.

A writ of habeas corpus is a request by a prisoner to have the government justify the detention. When a writ is issued, the officer or government authority is required to articulate the legal reasons the prisoner is being held. Habeas corpus means "you have the body" and is a protection against arbitrary arrests and unlawful and indefinite detainment. Such writs may only be suspended in cases of rebellion or invasion.

No bill of attainder or ex post facto law may be passed. A bill of attainder is an act of legislation that seeks to punish an individual or groups of individuals without the benefit of due process, such as a fair, speedy, and public trial with the assistance of an attorney, along with the opportunity to confront any witnesses. An ex post facto law is legislation that seeks to retroactively make certain conduct criminal or to increase criminal sanctions.

Capitations or "head taxes," along with other direct taxes, must be allocated according to the population of the states. Direct taxes are primarily taxes on property. The Sixteenth Amendment's imposition of the income tax created an exception to this requirement.

No Tax or Duty shall be laid on Articles exported from any State.

No Preference shall be given by any Regulation of Commerce or Revenue to the Ports of one State over those of another; nor shall Vessels bound to, or from, one State, be obliged to enter, clear, or pay Duties in another.

No Money shall be drawn from the Treasury, but in Consequence of Appropriations made by Law; and a regular Statement and Account of the Receipts and Expenditures of all public Money shall be published from time to time.

No Title of Nobility shall be granted by the United States: And no Person holding any Office of Profit or Trust under them, shall, without the Consent of the Congress, accept of any present, Emolument, Office, or Title, of any kind whatever, from any King, Prince, or foreign State.

No export tax may be imposed on goods going from one state to another. Compare to Article I, Section 8, which allows Congress to collect taxes, duties, imposts, and excises.

In the process of regulating commerce or trade, Congress may not give preference to the ports of one state over those in other states. In addition, vessels cannot be forced to pay for entry (tribute) or exit (clearance) from any port or to pay duties on their vessels. This prohibition was designed to ensure free movement from port to port and the avoidance of trade wars.

No money may be removed from the national treasury unless it has been legally approved by the elected representatives. Any money that is spent must be properly recorded and published.

The US government is prohibited from granting titles of nobility. The president and other US officials are forbidden from accepting gifts, perks, offices, or titles from foreign governments without permission from Congress. These restrictions are in place to prevent the United States from being influenced by foreign governments and to avoid the creation of an aristocratic or privileged class of individuals.

SECTION. 10.

No State shall:

enter into any Treaty, Alliance, or Confederation;

grant Letters of Marque and Reprisal;

coin Money; emit Bills of Credit; make any Thing but gold and silver Coin a Tender in Payment of Debts;

pass any Bill of Attainder, ex post facto Law, or Law impairing the Obligation of Contracts, or grant any Title of Nobility.

Section 10 (State Prohibitions on Legislation)

Some of the following powers, which are specifically prohibited to the states, are powers that are granted to the federal government through Article I, Section 8.

No state may enter into a treaty, alliance, or confederation with other states or foreign entities. This power is specifically granted to the federal government through Article II, Section 2 (Making of treaties by the president) and Article I, Section 8 (Ratification by the Senate).

No state may grant letters of marque and reprisal (giving a private entity power to engage in an act of war or retaliation against the enemy). This power is specifically granted to the federal government through Article I, Section 8.

No state may coin money or issue bills of credit or paper money. The separate states are to have no power over the medium to be used as legal tender in various commercial transactions. This power is specifically granted to the federal government through Article I, Section 8.

No bill of attainder or ex post facto law may be passed. A bill of attainder is an act of legislation that seeks to punish an individual or groups of individuals without the benefit of due process. An ex post facto law is legislation that seeks to retroactively criminalize certain conduct or increase criminal sanctions. The states are prohibited from infringing upon or voiding legally binding contracts between two or more parties. The states are prohibited from granting titles of nobility, which restriction is designed to prevent the creation of an aristocratic or privileged class of individuals.

No State shall, without the Consent of the Congress, lay any Imposts or Duties on Imports or Exports, except what may be absolutely necessary for executing it's inspection Laws: and the net Produce of all Duties and Imposts, laid by any State on Imports or Exports, shall be for the Use of the Treasury of the United States; and all such Laws shall be subject to the Revision and Controul of the Congress.

No State shall, without the Consent of Congress, lay any Duty of Tonnage, keep Troops, or Ships of War in time of Peace, enter into any Agreement or Compact with another State, or with a foreign Power, or engage in War, unless actually invaded, or in such imminent Danger as will not admit of delay.

Notes

Without the consent of Congress, the several states are prohibited from taxing and regulating exports and imports except to the extent to which it may be necessary under the states' inspection laws. In those cases where the states are permitted by Congress to tax imports or exports, any monetary gain that is realized through taxation is for the use of the federal government. Finally, Congress has the ultimate authority over trade with other nations and other states.

Without the consent of Congress, no state may do any of the following:
1. Issue tonnage duties, which are taxes directly related to the size of the ship.
2. Enter into interstate compacts or agreements with foreign entities.
3. Maintain a standing army and make war, except in case of invasion or imminent danger that requires immediate action. Note that Article IV specifically places the responsibility of protecting against state invasion on the federal government.

Article. II.

SECTION. 1.

The executive Power shall be vested in a President of the United States of America. He shall hold his Office during the Term of four Years, and, together with the Vice President, chosen for the same Term, be elected, as follows:

Each State shall appoint, in such Manner as the Legislature thereof may direct, a Number of Electors, equal to the whole Number of Senators and Representatives to which the State may be entitled in the Congress: but no Senator or Representative, or Person holding an Office of Trust or Profit under the United States, shall be appointed an Elector.

The Electors shall meet in their respective States, and vote by Ballot for two Persons, of whom one at least shall not be an Inhabitant of the same State with themselves.

And they shall make a List of all the Persons voted for, and of the Number of Votes for each; which List they shall sign and certify, and transmit sealed to the Seat of the Government of the United States, directed to the President of the Senate.

Article II
(POWERS OF THE EXECUTIVE BRANCH)

SECTION I (EXECUTIVE POWERS VESTED IN THE PRESIDENT)

The executive branch has the duty to enforce the law. The entirety of the executive power is vested in the president, and the president serves four-year terms. While there were originally no term limits, the Twenty-second Amendment bars an individual from serving more than two four-year consecutive terms. The president and vice president are to be elected at the same time, and according to the Twentieth Amendment, the term begins on January 20. The election process is to occur according to the following procedure:

Each state appoints electors, equal to the number of its congressional delegation (Senate and House of Representatives), who then vote for president. No person who holds federal office, including any member of Congress, is allowed to serve as an elector. The Twenty-third Amendment allows Washington, DC to also appoint electors along with the states.

The electors must meet in each of their states and vote for two people—namely, the president and the vice president. At least one of the two individuals they vote for may not reside in the same state as the electors. This requirement was changed by the Twelfth Amendment.

The electors must make a list of the individuals they voted for as president and another list of the individuals they voted for as vice president. The specific number of votes each candidate received must be included in this list. Each elector must sign and certify the list and then securely transmit

The President of the Senate shall, in the Presence of the Senate and House of Representatives, open all the Certificates, and the Votes shall then be counted. The Person having the greatest Number of Votes shall be the President, if such Number be a Majority of the whole Number of Electors appointed;

and if there be more than one who have such Majority, and have an equal Number of Votes, then the House of Representatives shall immediately chuse by Ballot one of them for President; and if no Person have a Majority, then from the five highest on the List the said House shall in like Manner chuse the President. But in chusing the President, the Votes shall be taken by States, the Representation from each State having one Vote; A quorum for this purpose shall consist of a Member or Members from two thirds of the States, and a Majority of all the States shall be necessary to a Choice.

In every Case, after the Choice of the President, the Person having the greatest Number of Votes of the Electors shall be the Vice President. But if there should remain two or more who have equal Votes, the Senate shall chuse from them by Ballot the Vice President.

The Congress may determine the Time of chusing the Electors, and the Day on which they shall give their Votes; which Day shall be the same throughout the United States.

this list to the president of the Senate. This requirement was changed by the Twelfth Amendment.

Once the votes are received from the respective states, the president of the Senate must open the lists in the presence of the Senate and the House of Representatives and count the votes. The person receiving the most votes shall be named the president so long as the proclaimed winner receives a simple majority of the total number of votes cast by the electors. This requirement was changed by the Twelfth Amendment.

In the event of a tie between two persons, the House of Representatives must decide by ballot who will be the president. In the event that no person receives a majority of the votes, the House of Representatives must choose from the five individuals with the most electoral votes. However, the votes must be taken by state, each state having one vote. A quorum of the House of Representatives must be present from each state in order to cast a vote. A quorum must consist of at least two-thirds of the members. A majority of all states must cast a vote in order for the vote to be final. This requirement was changed by the Twelfth Amendment.

The person receiving the most electoral votes will be president, and the person receiving the second greatest number of votes will be the vice president. If there are two or more individuals who, by way of a tie, have received the second greatest number of votes, the Senate will choose by ballot from those individuals. This requirement was changed by the Twelfth Amendment.

Congress may choose the day and time the electors are to meet and cast their votes. The date and time selected must be the same throughout the United States.

No Person except a natural born Citizen, or a Citizen of the United States, at the time of the Adoption of this Constitution, shall be eligible to the Office of President; neither shall any Person be eligible to that Office who shall not have attained to the Age of thirty five Years, and been fourteen Years a Resident within the United States.

<u>In Case of the Removal of the President from Office, or of his Death, Resignation, or Inability to discharge the Powers and Duties of the said Office, the Same shall devolve on the Vice President,</u>

and the Congress may by Law provide for the Case of Removal, Death, Resignation or Inability, both of the President and Vice President, declaring what Officer shall then act as President, and such Officer shall act accordingly, until the Disability be removed, or a President shall be elected.

The President shall, at stated Times, receive for his Services, a Compensation, which shall neither be increased nor diminished during the Period for which he shall have been elected, and he shall not receive within that Period any other Emolument from the United States, or any of them.

Before he enter on the Execution of his Office, he shall take the following Oath or Affirmation:--"I do solemnly swear (or affirm) that I will faithfully execute the Office of President of the United States, and will to the best of my Ability, preserve, protect and defend the Constitution of the United States."

In order to be eligible for the presidency of the United States, a person must be a natural born citizen or a citizen of the United States at the time of the Constitution's adoption. A person must also be at least thirty-five years old and a resident of the United States for no less than fourteen years.

If the president is removed from office through impeachment, death, resignation, or any other reason, the vice president will assume the duties of the presidency. <u>This requirement was changed by the Twenty-fifth Amendment.</u>

Congress may, through legislation, determine who succeeds to the presidency in the event that both the president and vice president are unable to discharge the duties of the presidency. Whoever is selected to act in that capacity will act as president until either the president is able to resume his or her duties or until a new president is elected.

The president must be paid a fixed salary for his or her services. However, the level of pay may not be increased or decreased during the president's term of office. The president may not receive any additional compensation from the national treasury or from the respective states.

Before assuming the office of the presidency and exercising executive authority, the president must take the following oath or affirmation: "I do solemnly swear (or affirm) that I will faithfully execute the Office of President of the United States, and will to the best of my Ability, preserve, protect and defend the Constitution of the United States." This oath is traditionally administered by the chief justice of the US Supreme Court. The phrase "so help me God," which is often stated as a part of the oath, was added by George Washington.

SECTION. 2.

The President shall be Commander in Chief of the Army and Navy of the United States, and of the Militia of the several States, when called into the actual Service of the United States;

he may require the Opinion, in writing, of the principal Officer in each of the executive Departments, upon any Subject relating to the Duties of their respective Offices, and he shall have Power to grant Reprieves and Pardons for Offences against the United States, except in Cases of Impeachment.

He shall have Power, by and with the Advice and Consent of the Senate, to make Treaties, provided two thirds of the Senators present concur; and he shall nominate, and by and with the Advice and Consent of the Senate, shall appoint Ambassadors, other public Ministers and Consuls, Judges of the supreme Court, and all other Officers of the United States, whose Appointments are not herein otherwise provided for, and which shall be established by Law: but the Congress may by Law vest the Appointment of such inferior Officers, as they think proper, in the President alone, in the Courts of Law, or in the Heads of Departments.

Section 2 (Powers of the Executive)

The president is the commander in chief and has the power to control the military forces of the United States during war and peacetime. The president also has power to control the military forces of the respective states when they are called into national service under Article I, Section 8.

As the one who presides over the executive branch and the various departments, the president may rely upon and request written opinions of the various cabinet members regarding their job function or anything related to the execution of their duties under the executive branch. The president also has the power to grant pardons (i.e., suspend or mitigate the imposed sentence) and reprieves (i.e., delay the implementation of a sentence) for offenses committed against the United States (i.e., in violation of federal law). The only offense for which a pardon is forbidden is impeachment.

The president has the power to negotiate and establish agreements with foreign nations upon the advice and consent of the Senate. In order for a treaty to have the force of law, two-thirds of the Senate must ratify. The president has the power to appoint judges, various administrators for the executive branch, and diplomatic officers such as ambassadors, ministers, and consuls. Those appointments will take place only upon the consent of the Senate. However, Congress does have the power to allow the president, judges, or other administrators to appoint officers without engaging in the confirmation process.

The President shall have Power to fill up all Vacancies that may happen during the Recess of the Senate, by granting Commissions which shall expire at the End of their next Session.

Notes

The president has the power to make temporary appointments to fill any vacancies while the Senate is in recess. Any temporary appointments will expire at the end of the next Senate session. If the president desires the appointee to retain the position, the appointee must undergo the senate confirmation process.

Notes

_____

_____

_____

_____

_____

_____

_____

_____

_____

_____

_____

_____

_____

_____

_____

_____

SECTION. 3.

He shall from time to time give to the Congress Information of the State of the Union, and recommend to their Consideration such Measures as he shall judge necessary and expedient;

he may, on extraordinary Occasions, convene both Houses, or either of them, and in Case of Disagreement between them, with Respect to the Time of Adjournment, he may adjourn them to such Time as he shall think proper;

he shall receive Ambassadors and other public Ministers;

he shall take Care that the Laws be faithfully executed,

and shall Commission all the Officers of the United States.

SECTION 3 (REPORTING STATE OF THE UNION, RESOLVING CONGRESSIONAL DISAGREEMENTS, DIPLOMATIC RELATIONS, AND FAITHFUL EXECUTION OF THE LAWS)

The president must on occasion appear before Congress and give a "State of the Union" address, in which he or she reports serious issues facing the nation and suggests a potential plan of action. Traditionally, the president delivers the State of the Union before a joint session of Congress in January.

If circumstances warrant it, the president may convene a special congressional session. Historically, the president has never called a special session, primarily because Congress meets nearly year round. If Congress disputes the time of adjournment among themselves, the president may intervene and establish the time of adjournment.

The president has the sole power to engage in diplomatic relations with foreign countries. The power to receive ambassadors and other public ministers equates to the power to determine the propriety of dealing with foreign countries and their assigned diplomats. Communication with other countries is important for purposes of trade, protection, etc., and this power lies primarily with the executive branch.

The president must ensure that the law is properly, consistently, and faithfully enforced. This clause, also known as the "take care" clause, allows the president to establish the manner in which laws will be enforced and his various executive duties will be carried out.

Even when the president's nominations for various executive appointments move through the senate confirmation process, the president still must deliver the commission, which grants the authority to act within a particular executive position.

SECTION. 4.

The President, Vice President and all civil Officers of the United States, shall be removed from Office on Impeachment for, and Conviction of, Treason, Bribery, or other high Crimes and Misdemeanors.

SECTION 4 (IMPEACHMENT)

The House of Representatives has the sole power of impeachment (Article I, Section 2), and the Senate has the sole power to hear and adjudicate the impeachment proceeding (Article I, Section 3). The president, vice president, or civil officers may be removed from office on the grounds of treason, bribery, or other high crimes and misdemeanors. Members of Congress are not deemed "civil officers" for purposes of this provision. However, Congress may remove its own members for misconduct upon a two-thirds vote (Article I, Section 5). The ultimate "impeachment" is by voters via the ballot box.

Notes

Article III.

SECTION. 1.

The judicial Power of the United States shall be vested in one supreme Court, and in such inferior Courts as the Congress may from time to time ordain and establish. The Judges, both of the supreme and inferior Courts, shall hold their Offices during good Behaviour, and shall, at stated Times, receive for their Services a Compensation, which shall not be diminished during their Continuance in Office.

Article III
(POWERS OF THE JUDICIAL BRANCH)

SECTION 1 (JUDICIAL AUTHORITY VESTED IN THE FEDERAL COURTS)

The judicial branch is the third branch of government and has the duty to interpret the law. This power is vested in the US Supreme Court (the highest court in the nation) and all inferior courts that Congress has power to establish via Article I, Section 8. The judges, who are appointed by the president (Article II, Section 2), hold their positions for life and are paid for their services, which may not be diminished during their term in office.

Note: Unlike the president and Congress, there are no age or citizenship requirements for judges.

SECTION. 2.

The judicial Power shall extend to all Cases, in Law and Equity, arising under this Constitution, the Laws of the United States, and Treaties made, or which shall be made, under their Authority;--to all Cases affecting Ambassadors, other public Ministers and Consuls;--to all Cases of admiralty and maritime Jurisdiction;--to Controversies to which the United States shall be a Party;--to Controversies between two or more States;-- between a State and Citizens of another State,--between Citizens of different States,--between Citizens of the same State claiming Lands under Grants of different States, and between a State, or the Citizens thereof, and foreign States, Citizens or Subjects.

In all Cases affecting Ambassadors, other public Ministers and Consuls, and those in which a State shall be Party, the supreme Court shall have original Jurisdiction. In all the other Cases before mentioned, the supreme Court shall have appellate Jurisdiction, both as to Law and Fact, with such Exceptions, and under such Regulations as the Congress shall make.

The Trial of all Crimes, except in Cases of Impeachment, shall be by Jury; and such Trial shall be

SECTION 2 (JURISDICTION OF THE FEDERAL COURTS)

The power to interpret the law lies with the US Supreme Court and all other lower courts, which Congress establishes via Article I, Section 8. The federal courts have the authority to hear civil and criminal cases that involve the US Constitution, federal law, or foreign agreements entered into by the president and ratified by Congress. Jurisdiction of the federal courts also extends to admiralty and maritime law (i.e., issues that originate on the high seas and that are subject to the law of nations). They also have jurisdiction over cases where the following entities are parties:

1. Various diplomats, such as ambassadors, public ministers, and consuls.
2. The United States.
3. Two or more states.
4. A state and a citizen (changed by the Eleventh Amendment).
5. Citizens of different states.
6. Citizens of the same state disputing lands granted by a state other than their own.
7. A state or its citizens and a foreign state and its citizens or subjects.

In all cases in which diplomatic officers (ambassadors, public ministers, and consuls) or a state is a party to a law suit, the US Supreme Court will have original jurisdiction. Original jurisdiction means the authority to hear the case upon first review as a trial court and not just as an appellate court. In all other cases, the US Supreme Court will act as an appellate court, in which it will review the decisions made by lower courts subject to any exceptions made by Congress.

With the exception of impeachment, all criminal cases enjoy the right to a jury trial. The location of the trial must

held in the State where the said Crimes shall have been committed; but when not committed within any State, the Trial shall be at such Place or Places as the Congress may by Law have directed.

Notes

_____

_____

_____

_____

_____

_____

_____

_____

_____

_____

_____

_____

_____

_____

_____

_____

take place within the state wherein the alleged crime occurred. If no state has jurisdiction over the particular commission of the crime, the venue will be subject to the determination of Congress. See the Sixth Amendment for more
information on jury trials and venue.

Notes

SECTION. 3.

Treason against the United States, shall consist only in levying War against them, or in adhering to their Enemies, giving them Aid and Comfort.

No Person shall be convicted of Treason unless on the Testimony of two Witnesses to the same overt Act, or on Confession in open Court.

The Congress shall have Power to declare the Punishment of Treason, but no Attainder of Treason shall work Corruption of Blood, or Forfeiture except during the Life of the Person attainted.

SECTION 3 (TREASON)

In order to be convicted of treason, the government must prove that the suspect:
1. waged war against the United States; or
2. supported the enemy by giving them aid and comfort.

In order to sustain a conviction for treason, there must be:
1. the testimony of two witnesses who testify as to the same act; or
2. a confession in open court.

Note: The accused continues to have the many rights secured through the Fifth Amendment (right to avoid compelled testimony) and the Sixth Amendment (fair trial, jury trial, speedy trial, confrontation of witnesses, and compelled appearance of the accused's witnesses).

Congress has the authority to determine the proper punishment for treason. However, any imposed punishment may not punish the traitor's heirs or family members. So, while the assets of the convicted traitor may be taken during the life of the accused, the inheritance of the traitor's property cannot be revoked.

Article. IV.

SECTION. 1.

Full Faith and Credit shall be given in each State to the public Acts, Records, and judicial Proceedings of every other State. And the Congress may by general Laws prescribe the Manner in which such Acts, Records and Proceedings shall be proved, and the Effect thereof.

Article IV
(RELATIONSHIPS AMONG THE STATES)

SECTION 1 (FULL FAITH AND CREDIT)

The "full faith and credit" clause requires that the respective states honor each other's civil laws, records, and court rulings. Specifically, if a judgment or legal order is issued in one state, other states are required to respect those judgments. For example, if an individual loses a lawsuit in Arizona, California must still enforce the judgment even though the judgment was issued outside of its jurisdiction. States are permitted to establish certain public policies, which are considered to fit outside the scope of the "full faith and credit" mandate. Public policy issues pertaining to marriage, for example, are an exception to the "full faith and credit" requirement. Congress is permitted to establish standards to validate and prove such official acts, as well as regulate "the effect thereof."

SECTION. 2.

The Citizens of each State shall be entitled to all Privileges and Immunities of Citizens in the several States.

A Person charged in any State with Treason, Felony, or other Crime, who shall flee from Justice, and be found in another State, shall on Demand of the executive Authority of the State from which he fled, be delivered up, to be removed to the State having Jurisdiction of the Crime.

No Person held to Service or Labour in one State, under the Laws thereof, escaping into another, shall, in Consequence of any Law or Regulation therein, be discharged from such Service or Labour, but shall be delivered up on Claim of the Party to whom such Service or Labour may be due.

SECTION 2 (PRIVILEGES AND IMMUNITIES, EXTRADITION, AND THE TREATMENT OF FUGITIVE SLAVES)

States are prohibited from infringing on the privileges and liberties of their own citizens or the citizens of other states without justification or due process. Rights which are preserved and protected for the citizens of one state must be preserved and protected for all. Compare to the Fourteenth Amendment's Privileges and Immunities clause.

This clause allows for what is commonly known as extradition. If a person is charged or convicted of a crime in one state and flees that state, the governor of the state in which the person has been charged or convicted of a crime may demand the custody and transport of the fugitive.

The "fugitive slave" clause allowed slaveholders or their agents to go into free states to capture slaves who had escaped the slaveholder's custody. This provision became obsolete as a result of the Thirteenth Amendment's ban on slavery.

SECTION. 3.

New States may be admitted by the Congress into this Union; but no new State shall be formed or erected within the Jurisdiction of any other State; nor any State be formed by the Junction of two or more States, or Parts of States, without the Consent of the Legislatures of the States concerned as well as of the Congress.

The Congress shall have Power to dispose of and make all needful Rules and Regulations respecting the Territory or other Property belonging to the United States; and nothing in this Constitution shall be so construed as to Prejudice any Claims of the United States, or of any particular State.

Section 3 (State Admission into the Union and Governance of US Property)

Congress must authorize the admission of any new state into the Union. However, no new state may be formed from or established within the jurisdiction of another state without the consent of the already-existing state legislature. Historically, admission has proceeded in the following manner:

1. Citizens of the territory must petition the federal government.
2. Upon receiving the petition, the president and Congress authorize the territory to draft a state constitution.
3. The proposed state constitution must be approved by a majority of both houses and by the president.
4. The territory is admitted as a new state in the Union.

Congress has the exclusive authority to determine the disposition and management, through any rules and regulations, of any land or property belonging to the United States. Nothing in the Constitution hinders any potential, unresolved legal claim to land by the respective states or the federal government.

SECTION. 4.

The United States shall guarantee to every State in this Union a Republican Form of Government, and shall protect each of them against Invasion; and on Application of the Legislature, or of the Executive (when the Legislature cannot be convened), against domestic Violence.

_____

_____

_____

_____

_____

_____

_____

_____

_____

_____

_____

_____

SECTION 4 (REPUBLICAN FORM OF GOVERNMENT)

Every state is guaranteed a republican form of government, which is to ensure that the rights of all people are protected, not just those that the majority believe are the most important, and to maintain the process of freely-elected representation. The federal government must protect each state from invasion. In cases of domestic violence or insurrection where the state believes assistance is necessary, the state experiencing the uprising or invasion must petition Congress or the president (in cases when Congress is not in session). Article I, Section 10 specifically prohibits the states from engaging in war unless the state is being invaded.

Note: Neither the Declaration of Independence nor the Constitution mentions the word democracy. Instead, the intent was to establish and maintain a republic.

Notes

_____

_____

_____

_____

_____

_____

_____

Article. V.

The Congress, whenever two thirds of both Houses shall deem it necessary, shall propose Amendments to this Constitution, or, on the Application of the Legislatures of two thirds of the several States, shall call a Convention for proposing Amendments,

which, in either Case, shall be valid to all Intents and Purposes, as Part of this Constitution, when ratified by the Legislatures of three fourths of the several States, or by Conventions in three fourths thereof, as the one or the other Mode of Ratification may be proposed by the Congress;

Provided that no Amendment which may be made prior to the Year One thousand eight hundred and eight shall in any Manner affect the first and fourth Clauses in the Ninth Section of the first Article; and that no State, without its Consent, shall be deprived of its equal Suffrage in the Senate.

Article V
(AMENDMENT PROCESS)

Amendments to the Constitution may be proposed in one of two ways:
1. Approval of two-thirds of both the House of Representatives and the Senate; or
2. Two-thirds of the states through their legislatures petition Congress to call for a constitutional convention.

Upon ratification, the amendment will become a part of the Constitution. Ratification of amendments to the Constitution may occur in one of two ways, either of which is determined by Congress:
1. Three-fourths of the state legislatures; or
2. Three-fourths of state ratifying conventions.

There are three amendments that may not be added to the Constitution:
1. An amendment banning the slave trade before 1808. This is also prohibited under Article I, Section 9. The Thirteenth Amendment, ratified in 1865, made this provision obsolete.
2. An amendment changing the limitations on direct or capitation taxes addressed in Article I, Section 9. The Sixteenth Amendment, ratified in 1913, made this provision obsolete.
3. An amendment depriving any state equal representation in the Senate without the state's consent.

Article. VI.

All Debts contracted and Engagements entered into, before the Adoption of this Constitution, shall be as valid against the United States under this Constitution, as under the Confederation.

This Constitution, and the Laws of the United States which shall be made in Pursuance thereof; and all Treaties made, or which shall be made, under the Authority of the United States, shall be the supreme Law of the Land; and the Judges in every State shall be bound thereby, any Thing in the Constitution or Laws of any State to the Contrary notwithstanding.

The Senators and Representatives before mentioned, and the Members of the several State Legislatures, and all executive and judicial Officers, both of the United States and of the several States, shall be bound by Oath or Affirmation, to support this Constitution; but no religious Test shall ever be required as a Qualification to any Office or public Trust under the United States.

Article VI
(Federal Debt, Supreme Law of the Land, Oath of Office, and No Religious Test for Public Office)

The United States will still be responsible for any debts incurred or agreements made prior to the ratification of the Constitution.

The "supremacy" clause establishes the Constitution, federal law, and treaties as "the supreme law of the land." State judges must uphold the US Constitution, even if state laws or state constitutions conflict with it. Any treaties entered into by the United States must comply with the Constitution.

All US senators, members of the US House of Representatives, members of the respective state legislatures, and US and state executive and judicial officers must take an oath to support and uphold the US Constitution. No religious test may ever be required for qualification to any position in the United States government.

Article. VII.

The Ratification of the Conventions of nine States, shall be sufficient for the Establishment of this Constitution between the States so ratifying the Same.

Attest William Jackson Secretary

done in Convention by the Unanimous Consent of the States present the Seventeenth Day of September in the Year of our Lord one thousand seven hundred and Eighty seven and of the Independance of the United States of America the Twelfth In witness whereof We have hereunto subscribed our Names,

G°. Washington
Presidt and deputy from Virginia

Delaware
  Geo: Read
  Gunning Bedford jun
  John Dickinson
  Richard Bassett
  Jaco: Broom

Maryland
  James McHenry
  Dan of St Thos. Jenifer
  Danl. Carroll

Virginia
  John Blair
  James Madison Jr.

North Carolina
  Wm. Blount
  Richd. Dobbs Spaight
  Hu Williamson

South Carolina
  J. Rutledge
  Charles Cotesworth Pinckney
  Charles Pinckney
  Pierce Butler

Georgia
  William Few
  Abr Baldwin

Article VII
(RATIFICATION)

Once at least nine states have ratified the Constitution, it will take effect among the states that ratified it.

Attest William Jackson Secretary

The Constitution was written by the unanimous consent of the states present on September 17, 1787, which is also the twelfth year of independence of the United States. As witnesses, the following signed their names:

George Washington:
President and deputy from Virginia.

Delaware
>   Geo: Read
>   Gunning Bedford jun
>   John Dickinson
>   Richard Bassett
>   Jaco: Broom

Maryland
>   James McHenry
>   Dan of St. Thos. Jenifer
>   Danl. Carroll

Virginia
>   John Blair
>   James Madison Jr.

North Carolina
>   Wm. Blount
>   Richd. Dobbs Spaight
>   Hu Williamson

South Carolina
>   J. Rutledge
>   Charles Cotesworth Pinckney
>   Charles Pinckney
>   Pierce Butler

Georgia
>   William Few
>   Abr Baldwin

New Hampshire
  John Langdon
  Nicholas Gilman
  Massachusetts
  Nathaniel Gorham
  Rufus King

Connecticut
  Wm. Saml. Johnson
  Roger Sherman

New York
  Alexander Hamilton

New Jersey
  Wil: Livingston
  David Brearley
  Wm. Paterson
  Jona: Dayton

Pennsylvania
  B Franklin
  Thomas Mifflin
  Robt. Morris
  Geo. Clymer
  Thos. FitzSimons
  Jared Ingersoll
  James Wilson
  Gouv Morris

Notes

New Hampshire
    John Langdon
    Nicholas Gilman
    Massachusetts
    Nathaniel Gorham
    Rufus King

Connecticut
    Wm. Saml. Johnson
    Roger Sherman

New York
    Alexander Hamilton

New Jersey
    Wil: Livingston
    David Brearley
    Wm. Paterson
    Jona: Dayton

Pennsylvania
    B Franklin
    Thomas Mifflin
    Robt Morris
    Geo. Clymer
    Thos. FitzSimons
    Jared Ingersoll
    James Wilson
    Gouv Morris

Notes

_____

_____

_____

_____

_____

_____

_____

_____

_____

_____

The Bill of Rights
THE PREAMBLE TO THE BILL OF RIGHTS

Congress of the United States
begun and held at the City of New-York, on
Wednesday the fourth of March, one thousand seven
hundred and eighty nine.

THE Conventions of a number of the States, having at the time of their adopting the Constitution, expressed a desire, in order to prevent misconstruction or abuse of its powers, that further declaratory and restrictive clauses should be added: And as extending the ground of public confidence in the Government, will best ensure the beneficent ends of its institution.

RESOLVED by the Senate and House of Representatives of the United States of America, in Congress assembled, two thirds of both Houses concurring, that the following Articles be proposed to the Legislatures of the several States, as amendments to the Constitution of the United States, all, or any of which Articles, when ratified by three fourths of the said Legislatures, to be valid to all intents and purposes, as part of the said Constitution; viz.

ARTICLES in addition to, and Amendment of the Constitution of the United States of America, proposed by Congress, and ratified by the Legislatures of the several States, pursuant to the fifth Article of the original Constitution.

The Bill of Rights
THE PREAMBLE TO THE BILL OF RIGHTS

The United States Congress began the work in the city of New York to establish a Bill of Rights on Wednesday, March 4, 1789.

The conventions of the separate states, having adopted the US Constitution, were concerned about the governmental abuse, misuse, and misinterpretation of powers. As a result, further restrictive powers were required in order to instill the people's confidence in the institution of government.

The United States Senate and the House of Representatives gathered and, in compliance with Article V of the Constitution, hereby amend the Constitution. Two-thirds of both the Senate and the House of Representatives voted for ratification. As a result, three-fourths of the state legislatures must ratify in order for these amendments to officially become a part of the Constitution.

Three-fourths of the separate states through the separate state legislatures ratified these ten amendments according to Article V of the Constitution.

Note: The first ten amendments, also known as the Bill of Rights, were ratified on December 15, 1791.

Amendment I

Congress shall make no law respecting an establishment of religion, or prohibiting the free exercise thereof; or abridging the freedom of speech, or of the press; or the right of the people peaceably to assemble, and to petition the Government for a redress of grievances.

Notes

First Amendment
(RELIGION, SPEECH, PRESS, ASSEMBLY, AND PETITION THE GOVERNMENT FOR REDRESS OF GRIEVANCES)

Congress may not make any law or engage in any action that does any of the following:

1. Establishes or endorses any particular religion or gives preference to one religious denomination over another.
2. Prohibits the practice of one's religious beliefs and practices.
3. Infringes on the liberty to speak or express one's views.
4. Inhibits the ability to print one's views.
5. Prohibits groups of individuals from peacefully assembling.
6. Prevents people from seeking problem resolution and reparation through their government.

Note: While this provision appears to be absolute, the government has and can create reasonable restrictions on the right of the people to assemble, to practice their religion, and to express themselves through various mediums. As with any other right, reasonable restrictions revolve around the principle that a person's rights end where the infringement on another person's rights begins.

Amendment II

A well regulated Militia, being necessary to the security of a free State, the right of the people to keep and bear Arms, shall not be infringed.

Notes

Second Amendment
(THE RIGHT TO KEEP AND BEAR ARMS)

Because a well-organized and regulated militia is essential to preserving freedom, the government may not make any law that infringes on the ability of the people to personally keep and bear firearms or other defensive weapons.

Although one of the explicit purposes of this particular right revolves around maintaining and establishing a well-regulated and organized militia, the right to keep and bear arms does not rest on the establishment of a "well-regulated militia."

At the time this amendment was written, the word "militia" was used interchangeably to describe two different bodies of armed individuals:

1. A state-established and potentially federally-controlled militia, as outlined in Article I, Sections 8 and 10.
2. A militia, which is made up of all of the people of a state, who have an inherent right to protect themselves and guard against a tyrannical government. It is this type of militia that the Second Amendment speaks to.

Amendment III

No Soldier shall, in time of peace be quartered in any house, without the consent of the Owner, nor in time of war, but in a manner to be prescribed by law.

Third Amendment
(QUARTERING OF SOLDIERS IN PRIVATE HOMES)

During peacetime, the government may not harbor soldiers in the homes or private facilities of the people without the consent of the owner. During wartime, the government may house soldiers in private facilities so long as adequate procedures and laws govern such occupation.

Note: This amendment has never been litigated. As a result, this protection has never been made applicable to the states. See the "due process" clause of the Fourteenth Amendment for further clarification.

Notes

_____

_____

_____

_____

_____

_____

_____

_____

_____

Amendment IV

The right of the people to be secure in their persons, houses, papers, and effects, against unreasonable searches and seizures, shall not be violated, and no Warrants shall issue, but upon probable cause, supported by Oath or affirmation, and particularly describing the place to be searched, and the persons or things to be seized.

Fourth Amendment
(SEARCH, SEIZURE, AND WARRANT REQUIRE-MENTS)

The people have the right to be protected against unreasonable government search or seizure (detainment) of their persons, homes, private facilities, documents, and personal belongings. Stated differently, the people have a right to be left alone unless the government has compelling evidence that a crime has been committed and that the person, place, or thing they wish to confront possesses evidence of that crime. Further, the people have the right to avoid arbitrary and unreasonable seizures (temporary and prolonged detention) and searches of their persons or property.

Before government officials can search or seize persons, places, or things, they must receive a special judicial permission known as a warrant. The following conditions must be satisfied before a warrant can be issued:

1. The warrant must be supported by probable cause (i.e., compelling evidence obtained through logical inquiry that would lead a reasonable person to believe that a crime has been committed).
2. The warrant must list the specific location or person to be searched.
3. The warrant must list the specific things or persons to be searched for (general, free-for-all searches are presumptively unreasonable and unconstitutional).
4. The government official applying for the warrant must avow that the information contained therein is truthful and accurate to the best of his or her knowledge and belief.
5. A neutral and detached judge must review the warrant and determine independently whether probable cause exists for the search.

Notes

The Fourth Amendment does not require that a warrant accompany all searches and seizures. A few examples of searches that are considered reasonable and which do not require a warrant are as follows:

1. Search incident to an arrest.
2. Exigent circumstances (hot pursuit away from a crime, public safety, and destruction of evidence).
3. Automobile exception (law enforcement observation of contraband inside a vehicle during a traffic stop).
4. Consent (individual waives their right not to be searched).
5. Protective sweep (upon investigating a crime in a private facility, generally in response to some sort of exigent circumstances, police may perform a quick sweep of the facility to ensure that no other persons are present who could present a safety threat).
6. Abandoned property.

Notes

_____

_____

_____

_____

_____

_____

_____

_____

Amendment V

No person shall be held to answer for a capital, or otherwise infamous crime, unless on a presentment or indictment of a Grand Jury, except in cases arising in the land or naval forces, or in the Militia, when in actual service in time of War or public danger; nor shall any person be subject for the same offence to be twice put in jeopardy of life or limb; nor shall be compelled in any criminal case to be a witness against himself, nor be deprived of life, liberty, or property, without due process of law; nor shall private property be taken for public use, without just compensation.

Notes

Fifth Amendment
(GRAND JURY, DOUBLE JEOPARDY, SELF-INCRIMINATION, DUE PROCESS, AND EMINENT DOMAIN)

Grand Jury: In order to continue to hold an individual for a capital (punishable by death) or otherwise felonious crime, a grand jury must determine whether sufficient evidence exists to allow the government to move toward trial. An indictment is a formal declaration that reflects the grand jurors' belief that enough evidence exists for the government to move forward. This is a preliminary check by the people on the government. Exceptions to the mandate of pursuing a grand jury indictment may occur during time of war or public danger. Military tribunals are also exceptions.

Note: This right to have the evidence heard preliminarily by a grand jury has not been made applicable to state governments. Many states use preliminary hearings in lieu of grand jury proceedings. The grand jury mandate only applies to the federal government. See the "due process" clause of the Fourteenth Amendment for further clarification.

Double Jeopardy: Once a person has been charged, the facts have been adjudicated, and there has been a finding of not guilty by a judge or jury, the government is forbidden from trying that individual again for the same crime or on the same set of facts.

Self-Incrimination: The government may not force a person to testify against him or herself. In addition, any statement obtained from the accused must be proven to be voluntary and free from coercion. This protection stems from the presumption of innocence and the idea that a suspect cannot be forced to help the government build its case.

Notes

Note: The US Supreme Court has held that Miranda warnings are an important protection that lessens the likelihood of compelled statements. Miranda warnings, which inform a criminal suspect of his right of silence and counsel, are now required anytime a criminal suspect is in custody and subject to interrogation.

Due Process: The government may not deprive a person of life, liberty, or property without fair proceedings that afford the person certain protections. Some of these protections include the right to a fair, public, and speedy trial, the right to confront any witnesses used by the government to prove their case, the right to remain silent, and the presumption of innocence. See the Fourth, Sixth, Eighth, and Fourteenth Amendments for further clarification.

Eminent Domain: This provision is commonly known as "eminent domain" or the "takings" clause and forbids the government from taking private property unless two standards are met:
1. The property is being taken for public use; and
2. There is fair and equitable compensation.

Amendment VI

In all criminal prosecutions, the accused shall enjoy the right to a speedy and public trial, by an impartial jury of the State and district wherein the crime shall have been committed, which district shall have been previously ascertained by law, and to be informed of the nature and cause of the accusation; to be confronted with the witnesses against him; to have compulsory process for obtaining witnesses in his favor, and to have the Assistance of Counsel for his defence.

Notes

Sixth Amendment
(Speedy Trial, Public Trial, Impartial Jury, Venue, Informed of the Accusation, Confrontation, Compulsory Attendances of Witnesses, and Assistance of Counsel)

In all criminal cases, the accused shall enjoy the following rights:

1. The right to a speedy and public trial. Because of the presumption of innocence, a person has a right to a relatively quick resolution of their case which may occur by way of plea agreement or trial. If not, the charges must be dismissed. The accused is also guaranteed the right to a public trial in order to safeguard against government misconduct.

2. The right to an impartial, unbiased, and fair jury from the same jurisdiction where the crime is alleged to have occurred.

3. The right to have the case heard in the same jurisdiction where the crime is alleged to have occurred.

4. The right to be informed of the accusations made by the government in order to allow for an adequate defense.

5. The right to confront and cross-examine any and all accusers and witnesses in order to test the veracity of their statements.

6. The right to compel witnesses to testify or produce evidence on behalf of the accused.

7. The right to have legal counsel.

Note: "All criminal cases" has been interpreted such that it does not include "all" criminal cases. Most misdemeanor crimes such as speeding and jaywalking are not entitled to certain Sixth Amendment protections (i.e., jury trial and government-provided legal representation).

Amendment VII

In Suits at common law, where the value in controversy shall exceed twenty dollars, the right of trial by jury shall be preserved, and no fact tried by a jury, shall be otherwise re-examined in any Court of the United States, than according to the rules of the common law.

Notes

Seventh Amendment
(CIVIL JURY TRIAL)

In civil (non-criminal) disputes between private parties where the amount exceeds twenty dollars, the right to a jury trial is protected. In addition, judges are not permitted to overturn factual findings made by a jury, subject to circumstances established by law.

Note: This right has not been made applicable to the states. As a result, states are free to decide whether such a right should be afforded to its citizens. See the "due process" clause of the Fourteenth Amendment for further clarification.

Notes

_____

_____

_____

_____

_____

_____

_____

_____

_____

_____

Amendment VIII

Excessive bail shall not be required, nor excessive fines imposed, nor cruel and unusual punishments inflicted.

Notes

_____

_____

_____

_____

_____

_____

_____

_____

_____

_____

_____

_____

_____

_____

Eighth Amendment
(EXCESSIVE BAIL AND CRUEL AND UNUSUAL PUNISHMENT)

Excessive Bail: Under the United States judicial system, a person is entitled to the presumption of innocence. As a result, individuals cannot be punished prior to a determination of guilt. However, certain conditions of release can be imposed in order to ensure their appearance at various proceedings, up to and including trial. Where criminal charges are pending, the government cannot require excessive bail, money, or property of a person as security to obtain release from jail. Note that while this provision prohibits excessive bail, it does not prohibit non-bailable status for offenses such as capital murder.

Excessive Fines: While punishment may be appropriate for various criminal offenses, this provision bars excessive fines and, in essence, mandates that any fine imposed should fit the seriousness of the crime.

Cruel and Unusual Punishment: Cruel and unusual punishment may not be imposed as a criminal sanction. One suggested method by the courts to determine whether the imposed punishment falls within the scope of cruel and unusual punishment is to evaluate the following:

1. Whether the punishment shocks the general conscience of a civilized society;
2. Whether the punishment is unnecessarily cruel;
3. Whether the punishment goes beyond legitimate penal aims (i.e., does the punishment seek to punish or do something more?)

Amendment IX

The enumeration in the Constitution, of certain rights, shall not be construed to deny or disparage others retained by the people.

Ninth Amendment
(Unenumerated Rights)

The Constitution does not grant individual rights—it recognizes and protects them. The fact that specific rights are not listed in the Constitution does not mean those rights do not exist. At the time the Bill of Rights was written, one of the primary concerns was that such a list might imply those were the only rights to which the people were entitled. As a result, the Ninth Amendment was included, which protects the rights "retained by the people" but not specifically written down in the Constitution. Examples of non-enumerated rights include the right to marry, have children, and travel.

Notes

_____

_____

_____

_____

_____

_____

_____

_____

_____

_____

Amendment X

The powers not delegated to the United States by the Constitution, nor prohibited by it to the States, are reserved to the States respectively, or to the people.

Notes

_____

_____

_____

_____

_____

_____

_____

_____

_____

_____

_____

_____

_____

Tenth Amendment
(STATES' RIGHTS)

The first seven articles of the Constitution refer to the power given to the federal government. The Tenth Amendment reserves the powers that were not given to the federal government and ensures that those remain with the states and/or the people. Although the states had to give up many powers in order to create the new Constitution, the Tenth Amendment guaranteed that the individual states and the people would play an ongoing role in the government. While the states gave up some of their power in order to have a strong central government, they retained enough power to preserve their sovereignty and operate somewhat independently of the federal government.

Notes

Amendment XI

Passed by Congress March 4, 1794. Ratified February 7, 1795.

The Judicial power of the United States shall not be construed to extend to any suit in law or equity, commenced or prosecuted against one of the United States by Citizens of another State, or by Citizens or Subjects of any Foreign State.

_____

_____

_____

_____

_____

_____

_____

_____

_____

_____

Eleventh Amendment
(JUDICIAL POWER)

Passed by Congress on March 4, 1794, and ratified on February 7, 1795.

A state, without its consent, may not be sued by citizens of a foreign nation or another state.

Note: The Eleventh Amendment modified Article III, Section 2.

Notes

_____

_____

_____

_____

_____

_____

_____

_____

_____

_____

_____

Amendment XII

Passed by Congress December 9, 1803. Ratified June 15, 1804.

The Electors shall meet in their respective states and vote by ballot for President and Vice-President, one of whom, at least, shall not be an inhabitant of the same state with themselves;

they shall name in their ballots the person voted for as President, and in distinct ballots the person voted for as Vice-President, and they shall make distinct lists of all persons voted for as President, and of all persons voted for as Vice-President, and of the number of votes for each, which lists they shall sign and certify, and transmit sealed to the seat of the government of the United States, directed to the President of the Senate;

-- the President of the Senate shall, in the presence of the Senate and House of Representatives, open all the certificates and the votes shall then be counted; -- The person having the greatest number of votes for President, shall be the President, if such number be a majority of the whole number of Electors appointed;

and if no person have such majority, then from the persons having the highest numbers not exceeding three on the list of those voted for as President, the House of Representatives shall choose immedi-

Twelfth Amendment
(ELECTION OF THE PRESIDENT
AND VICE PRESIDENT)

Passed by Congress on December 9, 1803, and ratified on June 15, 1804.

The electors voting for the president and the vice president must meet in their respective states and must vote by ballot. At least one of the candidates (either for president or for vice president) must be a citizen of a different state than that of the electors casting their ballots.

The electors must use separate ballots to vote for the president and vice president. They must make separate lists for all of the people they voted for as president and another list for all of the people they voted for as vice president. They must include the number of votes each person received. Finally, they must sign and certify the lists and send them to the president of the US Senate.

Upon receipt, the president of the US Senate must open and count all of the votes in the presence of the Senate and the House of Representatives (joint session of Congress). The person having the most votes for president will be named as the president so long as the total number of electoral votes equals a majority.

If no person receives a majority vote, the House of Representatives must immediately elect the president by ballot. They may only choose from the three individuals receiving the most votes. In choosing the president, the House of Rep-

ately, by ballot, the President. But in choosing the President, the votes shall be taken by states, the representation from each state having one vote; a quorum for this purpose shall consist of a member or members from two-thirds of the states, and a majority of all the states shall be necessary to a choice.

And if the House of Representatives shall not choose a President whenever the right of choice shall devolve upon them, before the fourth day of March next following, then the Vice-President shall act as President, as in case of the death or other constitutional disability of the President.

The person having the greatest number of votes as Vice-President, shall be the Vice-President, if such number be a majority of the whole number of Electors appointed, and if no person have a majority, then from the two highest numbers on the list, the Senate shall choose the Vice-President; a quorum for the purpose shall consist of two-thirds of the whole number of Senators, and a majority of the whole number shall be necessary to a choice. But no person constitutionally ineligible to the office of President shall be eligible to that of Vice-President of the United States.

resentatives will vote by state delegations, and each state will have only one vote. For this purpose, a quorum will consist of at least one member from two-thirds of the states, and a majority of all states will be necessary for the election to be final.

If the House of Representatives does not choose the president in the case where there is no individual receiving the majority of votes by March 4, then the sitting vice president will become acting president until the president is chosen. Section 3 of the Twentieth Amendment changed this portion of the Twelfth Amendment. The Twentieth Amendment establishes January 20 as the new Inauguration Day for the president. It also states that if a president has not been chosen by the beginning of the new term, then the vice president elect—not the sitting vice president—will serve as acting president until a president is chosen.

The person having the most votes for vice president will be named as the vice president so long as the total number of electoral votes equates to a majority. If no person receives a majority vote, the Senate must elect the vice president by ballot. They may only choose from the three individuals receiving the most votes. For this purpose, a quorum will consist of at least one member from two-thirds of the states, and a majority of all senators will be necessary for the election to be final. A person who is ineligible to be president of the United States will be ineligible to be vice president.

Note: The Twelfth Amendment supersedes a portion of Article II, Section 1.

Amendment XIII

Passed by Congress January 31, 1865. Ratified December 6, 1865.

SECTION 1.

Neither slavery nor involuntary servitude, except as a punishment for crime whereof the party shall have been duly convicted, shall exist within the United States, or any place subject to their jurisdiction.

SECTION 2.

Congress shall have power to enforce this article by appropriate legislation.

Thirteenth Amendment
(ABOLITION OF SLAVERY)

Passed by Congress on January 31, 1865, and ratified on December 6, 1865.

SECTION 1

Slave labor and involuntary servitude is prohibited in the United States or in any of its territories or possessions, except as the punishment for an individual who has been convicted of a crime.

SECTION 2

Congress has power to enact legislation in order to ensure that the prohibition of slavery is enforced.

Note: The Thirteenth Amendment supersedes a portion of Article IV, Section 2.

Amendment XIV

Passed by Congress June 13, 1866. Ratified July 9, 1868.

SECTION 1.

All persons born or naturalized in the United States, and subject to the jurisdiction thereof, are citizens of the United States and of the State wherein they reside. No State shall make or enforce any law which shall abridge the privileges or immunities of citizens of the United States; nor shall any State deprive any person of life, liberty, or property, without due process of law; nor deny to any person within its jurisdiction the equal protection of the laws.

Notes

Fourteenth Amendment
(Citizenship, Privileges and Immunities, Due Process, and Equal Protection)

Passed by Congress on June 13, 1866, and ratified on July 9, 1868.

Section 1

The Fourteenth Amendment, Section 1 has four provisions:

1. **Citizenship:** This clause defines both national and state citizenship, which had previously been left to the states to decide. In Dred Scott v. Sandford (1857), the Supreme Court ruled that African Americans, whether free or slave, could not be citizens of the United States. The Fourteenth Amendment overturned this decision by defining citizenship. A person can become a citizen of the state in which they reside as well as the United States if they are (a) born or naturalized in the United States and (b) subject to the jurisdiction of the United States (i.e., owe an allegiance to the sovereign of the US).

2. **Privileges and Immunities:** The original intent of this provision was to apply the provisions in the Bill of Rights to the states. However, the Supreme Court has interpreted this provision to protect only the rights of national citizenship of each individual living in the separate states (e.g., voting and travel). Compare to Article IV of the Constitution.

3. **Due Process:** State governments may not deprive a person of their life, liberty, or property without fair proceedings that afford the person certain protections. Some of these protections include notice as to what the law is, the right to a fair, public, and speedy trial,

SECTION 2.

Representatives shall be apportioned among the several States according to their respective numbers, counting the whole number of persons in each State, excluding Indians not taxed. But when the right to vote at any election for the choice of electors for President and Vice-President of the United States, Representatives in Congress, the Executive and Judicial officers of a State, or the members of the Legislature thereof, is denied to any of the <u>male inhabitants</u> of such State, <u>being twenty-one years of age</u>, and citizens of the United States, or in any way abridged, except for participation in rebellion, or other crime, the basis of representation therein shall be reduced in the proportion which the number of such male citizens shall bear to the whole number of <u>male citizens twenty-one years of age</u> in such State.

the right to confront any witnesses used by the government to prove their case, the right to remain silent, and the presumption of innocence. See the Fourth, Fifth, Sixth, and Eighth Amendments for further clarification. In addition, the Constitution, as originally written, only applied to the federal government. One of the reasons behind the Fourteenth Amendment was to apply certain provisions in the Bill of Rights to the states. The "due process" clause has been used to decide which provisions in the Bill of Rights should apply to the states (i.e., selective incorporation).

4. **Equal Protection:** This provision prohibits discrimination (i.e., individuals who are similarly situated must be treated in a similar manner). If a law treats people differently, the government must demonstrate a compelling reason for the difference in treatment.

SECTION 2

Members of the House of Representatives must be apportioned among the separate states according to the number of persons within that state. The only exception is non-taxpaying American Indians. This provision modifies Article I, Section 2 of the Constitution by eliminating the "three-fifths" clause. The right to vote in a federal or state election may not be denied to any male who is at least twenty-one years old. The exclusive right of males to vote was changed by the Nineteenth Amendment. The voting age was reduced to eighteen years of age in the Twenty-sixth Amendment. The right to vote may not be infringed upon unless that person participated in the confederate rebellion or upon a criminal conviction. If a state denies any eligible voter the right to vote at a regular election for state or federal offices, that state's representation in Congress will be reduced proportionally. That reduction will be based on the number of voters who were denied the opportunity to vote in proportion to the whole number of men over the age of twenty-one in the state.

SECTION 3.

No person shall be a Senator or Representative in Congress, or elector of President and Vice-President, or hold any office, civil or military, under the United States, or under any State, who, having previously taken an oath, as a member of Congress, or as an officer of the United States, or as a member of any State legislature, or as an executive or judicial officer of any State, to support the Constitution of the United States, shall have engaged in insurrection or rebellion against the same, or given aid or comfort to the enemies thereof. But Congress may by a vote of two-thirds of each House, remove such disability.

SECTION 4.

The validity of the public debt of the United States, authorized by law, including debts incurred for payment of pensions and bounties for services in suppressing insurrection or rebellion, shall not be questioned. But neither the United States nor any State shall assume or pay any debt or obligation incurred in aid of insurrection or rebellion against the United States, or any claim for the loss or emancipation of any slave; but all such debts, obligations and claims shall be held illegal and void.

SECTION 5.

The Congress shall have the power to enforce, by appropriate legislation, the provisions of this article.

SECTION 3

No person who previously served in a government position and took an oath to support the Constitution and then later fought against the United States or gave aid and comfort to those who did may hold any federal office or state offices within the three branches of government. Congress may, on an individual case-by-case basis, remove this restriction by a two-thirds vote.

Note: Almost all government and military officials of the Confederacy had held similar offices in the government or military of the United States before the Civil War and had taken an oath to "protect and defend the Constitution of the United States against all enemies, foreign and domestic." This provision of the Fourteenth Amendment was directed specifically at these "oath breakers" and was intended to forever bar them from holding any public office in the newly-reconstituted Union.

SECTION 4

Any debt incurred by the Union during the Civil War is valid. These debts include the payment of pensions and payment for services to assist in suppressing the Confederate rebellion. However, neither the US government nor state governments will assume any debts incurred by the Confederacy. Finally, there will be no reimbursement to slaveholders for the emancipation of slaves, and any such obligations will be declared illegal and void.

SECTION 5

Congress has the authority to enforce these specific provisions through further legislation.

Amendment XV

Passed by Congress February 26, 1869. Ratified February 3, 1870.

SECTION 1.

The right of citizens of the United States to vote shall not be denied or abridged by the United States or by any State on account of race, color, or previous condition of servitude--

SECTION 2.

The Congress shall have the power to enforce this article by appropriate legislation.

Notes

_____

_____

_____

_____

_____

_____

_____

Fifteenth Amendment
(Voting Rights: Race, Color, and Slave Status)

Passed by Congress on February 26, 1869, and ratified on February 3, 1870.

Section 1

The federal government or the separate states may not infringe upon the right to vote on the basis of race, color, or former slave status.

Section 2

Congress has the authority to enforce this specific protection through further legislation.

Notes

Amendment XVI

Passed by Congress July 2, 1909. Ratified February 3, 1913.

The Congress shall have power to lay and collect taxes on incomes, from whatever source derived, without apportionment among the several States, and without regard to any census or enumeration.

Sixteenth Amendment
(INCOME TAX)

Passed by Congress on July 2, 1909, and ratified on February 3, 1913.

Congress is permitted to collect taxes on income regardless of the income's source. This provision gave Congress an additional power even in spite of Article I, Sections 2, 8, and 9, which forbid direct taxes that are not assessed in proportion to the census.

Note: The Sixteenth Amendment modified Article I, Sections 2, 8, and 9.

Notes

_____

_____

_____

_____

_____

_____

_____

_____

_____

Amendment XVII

Passed by Congress May 13, 1912. Ratified April 8, 1913.

The Senate of the United States shall be composed of two Senators from each State, elected by the people thereof, for six years; and each Senator shall have one vote. The electors in each State shall have the qualifications requisite for electors of the most numerous branch of the State legislatures.

When vacancies happen in the representation of any State in the Senate, the executive authority of such State shall issue writs of election to fill such vacancies: Provided, That the legislature of any State may empower the executive thereof to make temporary appointments until the people fill the vacancies by election as the legislature may direct.

This amendment shall not be so construed as to affect the election or term of any Senator chosen before it becomes valid as part of the Constitution.

Seventeenth Amendment
(PEOPLE ELECT SENATORS)

Passed by Congress on May 13, 1912, and ratified on April 8, 1913.

The United States Senate is to be composed of two senators from each state, who will be elected by the people every six years. Every senator will have one vote in the Senate. Any person who is eligible to vote for a member of the largest branch of their state legislature is eligible to vote for a US Senator.

In the case of a vacancy in the Senate, the governor of the state from which the vacancy occurs must hold a special election to determine who will finish the remaining term. However, if the state legislature chooses to do so, it can allow the governor to make a temporary appointment until the special election is held.

This amendment will not affect the election or term of any senators who are serving at the time of the amendment's approval.

Note: The Seventeenth Amendment modifies Article I, Section 3 of the Constitution.

Amendment XVIII

Passed by Congress December 18, 1917. Ratified January 16, 1919. Repealed by amendment 21.

SECTION 1.

After one year from the ratification of this article the manufacture, sale, or transportation of intoxicating liquors within, the importation thereof into, or the exportation thereof from the United States and all territory subject to the jurisdiction thereof for beverage purposes is hereby prohibited.

SECTION 2.

The Congress and the several States shall have concurrent power to enforce this article by appropriate legislation.

SECTION 3.

This article shall be inoperative unless it shall have been ratified as an amendment to the Constitution by the legislatures of the several States, as provided in the Constitution, within seven years from the date of the submission hereof to the States by the Congress.

Eighteenth Amendment
(ALCOHOL PROHIBITION)

Passed by Congress on December 18, 1917, and ratified on January 16, 1919.

SECTION 1

One year after this amendment is ratified, it will be illegal to manufacture, sell, or transport intoxicating liquors into any state or territory of the United States. Both importation and exportation of alcoholic beverages into or out of any state or territory of the United States is also prohibited.

SECTION 2

Congress and the states have the power to enforce this prohibition through appropriate legislation.

SECTION 3

This amendment will not go into effect unless approved by the state legislatures, as outlined in Article V of the Constitution. Ratification must occur within seven years of passage by Congress.

Note: The Twenty-first Amendment repealed the Eighteenth Amendment.

Amendment XIX

Passed by Congress June 4, 1919. Ratified August 18, 1920.

The right of citizens of the United States to vote shall not be denied or abridged by the United States or by any State on account of sex.

Congress shall have power to enforce this article by appropriate legislation.

Nineteenth Amendment
(Voting Rights: Gender)

Passed by Congress on June 4, 1919, and ratified on August 18, 1920.

The right to vote may not be infringed upon by the federal government or the states on the basis of gender.

Congress has the authority to enforce this specific protection through further legislation.

Notes

_____

_____

_____

_____

_____

_____

_____

_____

_____

_____

_____

_____

Amendment XX

Passed by Congress March 2, 1932. Ratified January 23, 1933.

SECTION 1.

The terms of the President and the Vice President shall end at noon on the 20th day of January, and the terms of Senators and Representatives at noon on the 3d day of January, of the years in which such terms would have ended if this article had not been ratified; and the terms of their successors shall then begin.

SECTION 2.

The Congress shall assemble at least once in every year, and such meeting shall begin at noon on the 3d day of January, unless they shall by law appoint a different day.

SECTION 3.

If, at the time fixed for the beginning of the term of the President, the President elect shall have died, the Vice President elect shall become President. If a President shall not have been chosen before the time fixed for the beginning of his term, or if the President elect shall have failed to qualify, then the Vice President elect shall act as President until a President shall have qualified; and the Congress may by law provide for the case wherein neither a President elect nor a Vice President shall have qualified, declaring who shall then act as President, or the man-

Twentieth Amendment
(Inauguration and
Presidential Succession)

Passed by Congress on March 2, 1932, and ratified on January 23, 1933.

Section 1

The term of the president and vice president ends at noon on January 20, and the congressional term ends at noon on January 3. The successors of the president, vice president, and Congress will then begin their terms. The new Congress begins earlier than the president so that Congress has adequate time, if required as outlined in the Twelfth Amendment, to choose the president.

Section 2

Congress must meet at least once annually, and their meeting must begin on January 3. This provision changes Article I, Section 4, which mandated that the congressional session begin on the first Monday in December.

Section 3

If the president elect dies before the beginning of his or her term, the vice president elect will become the president. If the president has not been chosen or the elected president fails to qualify, the vice president will act as the president until one is chosen. Congress may determine by law further succession beyond the vice president. In the Presidential Succession Act of 1947, Congress established the order of presidential succession:

1. President
2. Vice president

ner in which one who is to act shall be selected, and such person shall act accordingly until a President or Vice President shall have qualified.

SECTION 4.

The Congress may by law provide for the case of the death of any of the persons from whom the House of Representatives may choose a President whenever the right of choice shall have devolved upon them, and for the case of the death of any of the persons from whom the Senate may choose a Vice President whenever the right of choice shall have devolved upon them.

SECTION 5.

Sections 1 and 2 shall take effect on the 15th day of October following the ratification of this article.

SECTION 6.

This article shall be inoperative unless it shall have been ratified as an amendment to the Constitution by the legislatures of three-fourths of the several States within seven years from the date of its submission.

3. Speaker of the House
4. President pro tempore of the Senate
5. Secretary of state
6. Remaining cabinet members according to the date of creation.

SECTION 4

The Twelfth Amendment provides that the House of Representatives chooses among the top three candidates for president if no candidate has a majority in the electoral college. In addition, the Senate chooses among the top two candidates for vice president if no candidate for that office has a majority in the electoral college. In the event that the House of Representatives or the Senate must choose a president or vice president, respectively, and one of the candidates happens to die, Congress may make a law to address the matter.

SECTION 5

Sections 1 and 2 will take effect on October 15 following approval of the amendment.

SECTION 6

This amendment will not go into effect unless approved by three-fourths of the state legislatures, as outlined in Article V of the Constitution. Ratification must occur within seven years of Congress sending it to the states.

Amendment XXI

Passed by Congress February 20, 1933. Ratified December 5, 1933.

SECTION 1.

The eighteenth article of amendment to the Constitution of the United States is hereby repealed.

SECTION 2.

The transportation or importation into any State, Territory, or Possession of the United States for delivery or use therein of intoxicating liquors, in violation of the laws thereof, is hereby prohibited.

SECTION 3.

This article shall be inoperative unless it shall have been ratified as an amendment to the Constitution by conventions in the several States, as provided in the Constitution, within seven years from the date of the submission hereof to the States by the Congress.

Twenty-first Amendment
(Repeal of the Eighteenth Amendment's Alcohol Prohibition)

Passed by Congress on February 20, 1933, and ratified on December 5, 1933.

Section 1

The Eighteenth Amendment is hereby repealed and will no longer carry with it the force of law.

Section 2

Intoxicating liquors may not be transported or imported into any state or territory of the United States if such transportation or importation violates that state's laws and if the liquors will be consumed in that state or territory.

Section 3

This amendment will not go into effect unless approved by the state legislatures, as outlined in Article V of the Constitution. Ratification must occur within seven years of Congress sending it to the states.

Amendment XXII

Passed by Congress March 21, 1947. Ratified February 27, 1951.

SECTION 1.

No person shall be elected to the office of the President more than twice, and no person who has held the office of President, or acted as President, for more than two years of a term to which some other person was elected President shall be elected to the office of President more than once. But this Article shall not apply to any person holding the office of President when this Article was proposed by Congress, and shall not prevent any person who may be holding the office of President, or acting as President, during the term within which this Article becomes operative from holding the office of President or acting as President during the remainder of such term.

SECTION 2.

This article shall be inoperative unless it shall have been ratified as an amendment to the Constitution by the legislatures of three-fourths of the several States within seven years from the date of its submission to the States by the Congress.

Twenty-second Amendment
(PRESIDENTIAL TERM LIMITS)

Passed by Congress on March 21, 1947, and ratified on February 27, 1951.

SECTION 1

No person may be elected president for more than two terms (four years per term). If a person serves more than two years of another president's term, he or she may only be elected for one additional term. Therefore, ten years is the maximum term any president can serve. This amendment will not apply to the any president or acting president serving at the time it is passed by Congress. In addition, if the amendment is approved, it will not prevent the president or acting president at the time of approval from finishing his or her term.

SECTION 2

This amendment will not go into effect unless approved by three-fourths of the state legislatures, as outlined in Article V of the Constitution. Ratification must occur within seven years of Congress sending it to the states.

Amendment XXIII

Passed by Congress June 16, 1960. Ratified March 29, 1961.

SECTION 1.

The District constituting the seat of Government of the United States shall appoint in such manner as Congress may direct:

A number of electors of President and Vice President equal to the whole number of Senators and Representatives in Congress to which the District would be entitled if it were a State, but in no event more than the least populous State; they shall be in addition to those appointed by the States, but they shall be considered, for the purposes of the election of President and Vice President, to be electors appointed by a State; and they shall meet in the District and perform such duties as provided by the twelfth article of amendment.

SECTION 2.

The Congress shall have power to enforce this article by appropriate legislation.

Twenty-third Amendment
(WASHINGTON, DC: SEAT OF GOVERNMENT)

Passed by Congress on June 16, 1960, and ratified on March 29, 1961.

SECTION 1

The District of Columbia is designated as the seat of government and the nation's capital.

Those individuals living in the District of Columbia have the opportunity to vote for the president and vice president at the regular elections. Congress will provide for the appointment of electors, which may consist of no more than the number of electors of the least populous state. The votes of these electors will count as if the District of Columbia were a state. The electors will meet in the District of Columbia and will perform their duties as outlined in the Twelfth Amendment.

SECTION 2

Congress has the authority to enforce this specific provision through further legislation.

Amendment XXIV

Passed by Congress August 27, 1962. Ratified January 23, 1964.

SECTION 1.

The right of citizens of the United States to vote in any primary or other election for President or Vice President, for electors for President or Vice President, or for Senator or Representative in Congress, shall not be denied or abridged by the United States or any State by reason of failure to pay poll tax or other tax.

SECTION 2.

The Congress shall have power to enforce this article by appropriate legislation.

Twenty-fourth Amendment
(Poll Tax Prohibition)

Passed by Congress on August 27, 1962, and ratified on January 23, 1964.

Section 1

The federal government and the separate states may not prohibit a citizen from voting for president, vice president, presidential and vice presidential electors, senator, or members of the House of Representatives because of a failure to pay any tax, including a poll tax.

Section 2

Congress has the authority to enforce this specific provision through further legislation.

Amendment XXV

Passed by Congress July 6, 1965. Ratified February 10, 1967.

SECTION 1.

In case of the removal of the President from office or of his death or resignation, the Vice President shall become President.

SECTION 2.

Whenever there is a vacancy in the office of the Vice President, the President shall nominate a Vice President who shall take office upon confirmation by a majority vote of both Houses of Congress.

SECTION 3.

Whenever the President transmits to the President pro tempore of the Senate and the Speaker of the House of Representatives his written declaration that he is unable to discharge the powers and duties of his office, and until he transmits to them a written declaration to the contrary, such powers and duties shall be discharged by the Vice President as Acting President.

SECTION 4.

Whenever the Vice President and a majority of either the principal officers of the executive departments or of such other body as Congress may by law provide, transmit to the President pro tempore of the Senate and the Speaker of the House of Representatives their written declaration that the President is unable to discharge the powers and duties of

Twenty-fifth Amendment
(PRESIDENTIAL SUCCESSION)

Passed by Congress on July 6, 1965, and ratified on February 10, 1967.

SECTION 1

In the case of removal, death, or resignation of the president, the vice president will become the president.

SECTION 2

In the case of a vacancy of the office of vice president, the president will appoint a vice president, subject to the consent of the majority of both the Senate and the House of Representatives.

SECTION 3

In cases where the president may be unable to carry out his or her powers and obligations, he or she must advise both the president pro tempore of the Senate and the speaker of the House of Representatives. The vice president will be the acting president until the president advises that he or she is once again capable of discharging his or her duties and obligations.

SECTION 4

The president can be temporarily removed from acting in his or her office if the vice president and a majority of the cabinet officers (or any other body designated by Congress) decide that he or she cannot fully discharge the duties of the office. In order to do this, the vice president and a majority of the cabinet members must submit a written statement to the president pro tempore of the Senate and the Speaker of

his office, the Vice President shall immediately assume the powers and duties of the office as Acting President.

Thereafter, when the President transmits to the President pro tempore of the Senate and the Speaker of the House of Representatives his written declaration that no inability exists, he shall resume the powers and duties of his office unless the Vice President and a majority of either the principal officers of the executive department or of such other body as Congress may by law provide, transmit within four days to the President pro tempore of the Senate and the Speaker of the House of Representatives their written declaration that the President is unable to discharge the powers and duties of his office. Thereupon Congress shall decide the issue, assembling within forty-eight hours for that purpose if not in session. If the Congress, within twenty-one days after receipt of the latter written declaration, or, if Congress is not in session, within twenty-one days after Congress is required to assemble, determines by two-thirds vote of both Houses that the President is unable to discharge the powers and duties of his office, the Vice President shall continue to discharge the same as Acting President; otherwise, the President shall resume the powers and duties of his office.

the House of Representatives expressing their belief that the president is not able to fulfill his or her duties. Upon the submission of this declaration, the vice president immediately assumes the powers and duties of the presidency as acting president.

To regain his or her powers, the president must submit a written declaration to the president pro tempore of the Senate and the Speaker of the House of Representatives, stating that no inability exists. The president shall immediately resume the powers of the presidency. However, if the vice president and a majority of the cabinet submit another letter to the same congressional leaders within four days stating that an inability still exists, the vice president will resume the powers of the presidency as acting president until Congress decides the matter. Congress has forty-eight hours to meet to decide the issue if they are not in session and has a total of twenty-one days to decide the issue once they are in session. If they decide by a two-thirds vote of both houses that the president is unable, the vice president continues to function as acting president. Otherwise the president resumes the powers and duties of his or her office.

Note: The Twenty-fifth Amendment modified Article II, Section 1 of the Constitution.

Amendment XXVI

Passed by Congress March 23, 1971. Ratified July 1, 1971.

SECTION 1.

The right of citizens of the United States, who are eighteen years of age or older, to vote shall not be denied or abridged by the United States or by any State on account of age.

SECTION 2.

The Congress shall have power to enforce this article by appropriate legislation.

Notes

_____

_____

_____

_____

_____

_____

_____

_____

_____

Twenty-sixth Amendment
(Right to Vote: Eighteen Years of Age)

Passed by Congress on March 23, 1971, and ratified on July 1, 1971.

Section 1

The right of citizens to vote who are eighteen years of age and older may not be infringed upon by the federal government or the states.

Section 2

Congress has the authority to enforce this specific protection through further legislation.

Note: The Twenty-sixth Amendment modified Section 2 of the Fourteenth Amendment.

Amendment XXVII

Originally proposed Sept. 25, 1789. Ratified May 7, 1992.

No law, varying the compensation for the services of the Senators and Representatives, shall take effect, until an election of representatives shall have intervened.

Twenty-seventh Amendment
(Congressional Pay)

Proposed on September 5, 1789, and ratified on May 7, 1992.

No law that changes the pay rate of senators and members of the House of Representatives will take effect until after an election of representatives has occurred.

Note: The First United States Congress in 1789, in response to the demands of several of the states' ratification conventions, proposed twelve amendments to the Constitution. Ten of these were ratified and became known as the Bill of Rights. The Twenty-seventh Amendment was one of the original twelve amendments submitted for ratification, but was not ratified until May 7, 1992. Had it been ratified with the Bill of Rights, it would have been the First Amendment.

AMERICA, RISE UP!
(AFTERWORD)

Our Constitution is the oldest in the world and is the model for proper government. Americans must rise up and recognize the great honor it is to be an American and return to the document that protects our liberty. America needs people of courage who comprehend the Constitution, American exceptionalism, and experience in their hearts and minds why we must make a case for the retention of the Constitution.

As Americans, we must do four things:
- Know and understand the Constitution;
- Recognize and live the principles of liberty upon which this Constitution was founded;
- Elect officials who understand the Constitution and its accompanying principles of liberty and don't just pay lip service to them; and
- Hold these officials accountable.

As you recognize how profound this document is, you will transition to analyzing issues first on their constitutionality. Once the constitutionality of the idea is established, you can then move on to discussing whether the idea is "good" or "bad" for America. Constitution first, merits second! This is the art of becoming a constitutional technician.

Together, we will restore this Constitution. Together, we will restore freedom. Together, we will restore America.

This is your nation to save.

Index

Acknowledgements

Countless important individuals have made this simple, yet profound, work possible. Thank you for motivating this work, for it is one of the many pieces of the solution to the problem that this great country faces.

To my wife, Janelle, for her endless motivation to become a true asset to America and to give back in ways that reflect our love for it. Without her, this work is nonexistent. Without her, I am unable to do the things I truly love. With her, I see America!

To my children, Ammon, Daniel, Jacob, Fenton, Aidan, and Shanelle, for their inquiring minds, patriotic spirit, and priceless love.

To my mother, Erna Arnold, and my father, Richard Arnold, for the endless debates around the dinner table and for helping me see how blessed we Americans truly are. This book is nothing less than a product of standing on their shoulders where I was able to see the things that so many take for granted.

To Margaret Andrews for making this happen and ensuring I kept on track. She has helped me better see my calling as an American and opened up countless doors. What a patriot with a firm, nonnegotiable foundation who understands what America needs and who sees the vision of truly restoring America!

To Douglas D. Brown for instilling confidence in this project and for creating numerous opportunities for me and the Academy to carry this important message forward.

To William "Bill" Bish, the living spirit of James Madison and a real example of what patriots used to do. He motivated and pushed this work forward non-stop and is the captain who constantly points the way. He consistently reminds me that "real change" is on the horizon.

To Sandra Udall Crandall, my lead editor, for being a tireless sounding board for my ideas and for so skillfully editing and refining this work.

To Susan Veach, the formatter and designer of this work, for her attention to detail and ensuring that the arrangement of this work met the highest of standards.

To E. Paul Whetten, Kevin Boswell, and Ken Diliberto for their fantastic contribution in the editing of this work and for helping ensure its accuracy.

To the thousands of people who have heard me speak and offered their unwavering support and encouragement. Thank you for your example of America in action and for inspiring this work.

About the Author

Shane F. Krauser is the director of the American Academy for Constitutional Education (AAFCE), an adjunct professor of constitutional and criminal law, a firearms instructor, and a practicing trial attorney. He has written extensively on the principles of freedom and the Constitution.

Mr. Krauser completed his undergraduate work at Arizona State University, where he graduated summa cum laude. Shortly thereafter, he graduated with his law degree (JD) from the University of Utah.

Mr. Krauser has been involved in numerous projects of constitutional import, including the Oklahoma City Bombing Trial, victims' rights legislation, and an attempt to overturn the Fifth Amendment's Miranda requirements argued before the U.S. Supreme Court (Dickerson v. United States). He has also worked as a felony prosecutor in Arizona, where he handled cases involving gang violence, homicide, armed robbery, aggravated assault, and home invasions. In 2004, Mr. Krauser received the Fordham Public Service Alumni Award from the University of Utah.

Mr. Krauser was born and raised in Arizona. He grew up in a family where the principles of human freedom and the exceptionalism of America were often debated and discussed. He has focused on carrying this tradition forward with his own family, as he recognizes the strength of this country lies in its youth and their understanding of liberty and history. Mr. Krauser and his beautiful wife, Janelle, are the parents of six children. They reside in Arizona, where they enjoy traveling, the outdoors, and being involved together in many community events.

Contact
For Book Sales, Speaking Engagements, and Seminars

Mr. Krauser is a widely sought-after speaker, has traveled the country speaking on countless issues pertaining to the Constitution and human freedom, and has been called by many the "best instructor on the Constitution in the country." He has spoken at political rallies, addressed large audiences at various political and corporate conventions, guided expert panels with various political figures, appeared on the radio, inspired students in both public and private schools, and educated audiences of all sizes and demographics. He brings a wealth of knowledge to any forum, and that knowledge will inspire you. His experiences will captivate you. His dedication will move you.

He is available to speak at any number of venues and may be contacted at Shane.Krauser@aafce.com. To order books, contact info@aafce.com or go to the website of the American Academy for Constitutional Education at www.aafce.com.